Strength of Character and Grace

Strength of Character and Grace

DEVELOP THE COURAGE TO BE BRILLIANT

MARTA MONAHAN

WITH JEFF ANDRUS

Vittorio.

LOS ANGELES

Visit our Web Site at www.vittoriomedia.com

Printed in the United States of America
First Printing: April 2000

Library of Congress Catalog Card Number
99-75863
ISBN 1-892409-13-5

FIRST EDITION

This book is printed on acid-free paper.

Book Design by Trina Stahl Design

The names and some of the circumstances of all clients and students herein
have been altered in order to preserve their confidentiality.

To the discovery of your essence,
that you recognize it, respect it,
and fall in love with it.

Contents

Introduction

I WAS BORN in El Salvador, the second of five children. My father was a man of distinction—a consul-general, a bank assessor and an advisor to presidents. He adored my mother, and she was devoted to him. They reared me in a proper manner, and I grew up surrounded by people of high principles who imparted wisdom to me, often by the example of simply being who they were and sometimes by conscious teaching. We lived in New York City for several years; I traveled some; I speak three languages. My adolescence was wholesome, uncomplicated and generally filled with joy.

Yet I have gone through my share of grief and suffering, including succumbing to my own poor decisions. I do not regret the difficulties or the consequences because they were excellent teachers that helped me understand that I am the accumulation of all my choices.

It was in the worst and in the best of times that I learned the principles that I have put in this book. They came as revelations gained by my own efforts and by interaction with people of caliber. One of these people was Pilar Garcia-Bailon, my friend and last mentor. We lectured and conducted seminars for corporations and government agencies for eleven years until Pilar died of cancer.

This book is about how each of us can live a courageous life of brilliance, enjoying success and dignity. Brilliance shines forth from adhering to basic moral and mental principles. We move toward brilliance by small choices that build strength of character. From strength of character come the threads, and eventually the tapestry of an outer life characterized by elegant and inspirational conduct. That is to say a life of uncommon grace.

I am on the road to brilliance as a student and a seeker, someone who is still striving to be whole. These are my credentials as a teacher. I began this career in 1975. I do not have a university degree, but I have taught people with five doctorates. I have taught people of all ages and from all walks of life—professionals, executives, politicians, diplomats, members of society, homemakers and laborers. They call, they write, they come to see me, and report extraordinary things unfolding in their private lives and at their places of work.

So quite naturally, I expect that as you read this book you will choose to do extraordinary things too.

Marta Monahan
Los Angeles, California

Strength of Character and Grace

Brilliance

PEOPLE LEAPT TO their feet around me to applaud, but I was frozen to my seat, appalled by my lack of enthusiasm.

The Bolshoi Ballet was in Los Angeles, and I was there as an eager member of the audience at its first performance of *Giselle.* I had seen *Giselle* many times in the past and always been charmed. Every routine looked precise, without mistakes and seemingly perfect. But something was missing. As the company received a standing ovation, I felt as if I had wasted my time and money.

I was only five years old when I was taken to my first ballet. I fell asleep for a good portion of what was happening on stage. After all I was a small child. But what I did see touched me so deeply I wanted to cry. The beauty of the music and dance awakened in me an appetite to seek similar kinds of sublime communion again and again.

So it was strange to be in the presence of one of the most famous ballet companies in the world and be untouched. It was not until the next morning when I read the review in the *Times* that I understood why. So many Soviet artists had defected to the West, the Bolshoi did not want to risk losing more. In self-preservation the company had sent understudies, performers who practiced for accuracy and repeated it. And repeated it.

Again and again.

Precisely without risk.

Coldly without soul.

Even a five-year-old senses when there is more. The more is when a dancer gives her best. Giving her best means starting with what she can do and taking the risk to go beyond, to stretch and do better. This is called excellence by many. It is like the brilliance of a diamond, something that comes naturally but has been worked on and polished until it shines with the light of perfection. Since my childhood encounter with brilliance in dance, I have seen it in ice skaters and in gymnasts. Its expressions are limitless and to be found in the words of a poet, in the mathematical notations of a physicist, in the ringing blows of a hammer in the hand of a master carpenter, in the selfless sacrifices of an Albert Schweitzer or a Mother Theresa, and in the countless activities that individuals decide to do with all of their hearts. Over the years I have come to be convinced of a fundamental fact of life: our natural instinct as human beings is to seek brilliance.

This instinct is nurtured by conscious commitment, or it is smothered and debased by others and us. In the larger world abusive or absent parents, mean streets and a legion of modern ills take a terrible toll against brilliance. Yet brilliance rises to the surface even in the worst of circumstances. Beethoven wrote 400 versions of the Fifth Symphony until he composed the brilliant one we hear today. Helen Keller rose above both deafness and blindness. Stephen Hawking and Christopher Reeve refuse to let wheelchairs handicap their commitment to brilliance.

Because brilliance will not be contained, striving to fulfill its potential in one facet of our lives causes us to discover new talents and build new skills that bring it into all other facets.

BRILLIANCE IS COMPASSION AND COURAGE

A LIFE OF BRILLIANCE is a life of wholeness. It is to be satisfied with material success and personal happiness, but not to stop there. It is to be fulfilled in sharing success—material, moral, intellectual and spiritual—with others. People living in brilliance grow in compassion and use accomplishments to spur them to further achievement. They do not know envy. Their companion is courage, and they are courageous enough to manifest love in terms of respect, patience and courtesy that draws excellence from others.

Each of us is born with the full equipment to be brilliant. In spite of difficulties that arise because of our own choices or those of others, we can make any situation better. Brilliant people enjoy the challenge of molding their characters toward higher good. They know that we can always approach perfection, and being on the approach means that we are in contact with the absolute at any time. In the infinite goodness of God's perfection there is no condemnation, only encouragement for each individual to find the unique truth of his own brilliance. Just as important, brilliant people are free from the pretense that they have to be as perfect as God himself.

They recognize that none of us is better than another. It is what we do or do not do with our lives that makes us different. Excellence can be achieved in art, in business, in personal habits, in any area, by any person regardless of his station in life. Insomuch as excellence is attained in one area of our lives, it becomes the means for attaining it in others and thereby fulfilling our highest destiny, a life of brilliance.

WHAT IS HOLDING US BACK?

BEING STUCK IN a situation or condition is such a common experience that people share it freely without embarrassment. Yet the moment we get stuck in some aspect, we stop growing. We start to lose appreciation for what we have accomplished and what we have become. Because we have an intuitive desire to manifest brilliance, we know we are settling for less. The shame of failure compels us to justify our circumstances with excuses. The challenge, then, is to look at our true condition with courage.

Consider a single situation in your life that is causing suffering to your person, in a relationship or with your work. You do not have to describe it, just give it a name so that in retrospect you will know what you were referring to. It is not uncommon for people to forget what their unsolved situation was after they move away from it. Do not be concerned if you have more than one. The same way of thinking will create the same circumstances in several situations at once.

Please stop to do this exercise now. To continue reading and come back to the exercise will dilute the impact. Take advantage of the moment and make the effort to begin to expand your thinking toward brilliance.

- Choose one unresolved situation in any area of your life.
- How old is the situation?
- How much time do you spend thinking about it on an average day?
- Multiply the daily average by 30 so that you get a monthly average. Multiply the monthly average by 12 to get your yearly average, and then multiply the result by the number of years that the situation has been unresolved.
- The above figure is prime time that could have been used in more constructive ways. Write down some areas in which you could have used this time to enhance your life.
- Ask yourself if the situation is better, worse or the same as when it began.
- Consider at least five negative emotions that you are living with as a result of this unresolved situation.

If you answered better to the question about the state of your situation since it began, you have spent some time trying to solve the problem.

If you answered worse, then you spent your time reliving the situation, justifying your choices, blaming and resenting others for something you probably now believe was not your doing or that you did not have any participation in. You have resigned yourself to the role of victim.

If you answered the same, you may feel relatively comfortable because at the very least your situation seems no worse. Sadly, you are still stuck. While things may look the same, they are not. They are in fact deteriorating, and so are you. Time does not resolve things. On the contrary, it alienates you from your solutions; it comes between you and your desires as you become weaker, angrier and more frightened with each day.

After careful review of your answers, ask yourself two final questions:

- What are five negative emotions that you will live with three, six or ten years from now if you do not resolve the situation? (These will be the same ones you noted earlier plus all of the ramifications of continued failure.)
- How does this unsolved situation affect your work, social or personal life?

Your answers above are painting a picture of your future. It is already crystallizing, waiting for you to meet it.

Whenever I do this exercise in lectures, I always ask if students will volunteer to read aloud their negative emotions. I see pain reflected in most faces. However, it is my blessing that at the end of the time spent together there is hope and determination on the same faces. We need to understand the cause-and-effect in our lives to fully grasp the seriousness of being stuck. Our clarity will produce an urgency to change the downward trend. Your situation may be unique, but you are not alone in your grief because the suffering is universal. Following are some of the common emotions gleaned from my experience and those of my participants. The same negative words consistently appear on the lists. All express the same way of thinking.

insecure	angry
resentful	fear
distracted	self-doubt
self-hate	irresponsible

impotent	weak
hopeless	revengeful
unmotivated	stagnant
lonely	depleted
depressed	frustrated
trapped	submissive
betrayed	humiliated
manipulated	abused
violated	low self-esteem
victimized	isolated
overwhelmed	guilty
envious	impatient
exhausted	cheated
short-tempered	inept
inadequate	cowardly
phony	bored
hurt	wounded

Most people do not see that being stuck is a problem until they do this exercise. Their reasoning is that all of us are stagnating in one aspect or another. Therefore their condition is normal, part of being "just average" and nothing to worry about. Yet it is a rare person who will profess a desire to be average.

THE LIMITATIONS OF BEING AVERAGE

SEVERAL YEARS AGO a friend asked me out to dinner so that I could speak to her twelve-year-old daughter. Colleen's grades were not bad, but they weren't good either. No matter how my friend had tried to motivate Colleen to do better, the girl had the same pat answer that closed further discussion.

"I'm just like everyone else. What's wrong with that? I'm happy being average."

I had known Colleen most of her young life, and we had earned each other's trust and affection. As we left for the restaurant, I began my usual conversation with Colleen, asking her about her friends, school, teachers, sports and any new activities with which she had become involved since our last visit. Then I asked about her grades.

"You've been talking to my mom," she said petulantly.

"Yes."

"Then," she said, "you already know that my grades are just fine. I'm not failing. I'm just like everybody else, and there is nothing wrong with being average either." The topic was clearly closed.

"I agree," I said, "there is nothing wrong with being average."

Colleen's eyes widened.

"However," I continued, "being average means settling for less in every area of your life. Right now you probably do not see that because your life is not average. Your mother makes efforts that allow her to provide you a lovely home. It is not in an average neighborhood. You do not eat average food. Everything you have is of high quality because your mother provides you with an environment that is very special. I know that she surrounds herself with people who are not average, and I know you enjoy participating in interesting conversations with them."

"But you'll find out someday what average means. It means mediocre. You might as well become familiar with the word now because that is what you have chosen to be." I directed the conversation to her mother because now it was my turn. Topic closed.

Colleen waited for a pause in the new conversation to ask me to tell her more about mediocrity.

"Accepting mediocrity now as a way of life means that you will probably be average for the rest of your life. You will have to accept average opportunities, take an average job and make average friends. Someday you may want to get married and have children, but it would be a mistake to get romantic ideas about an intelligent outstanding man because those kind of men want an above-average woman. But you will find yourself a nice average husband, and someday you will have average kids and a nice average life. Just like everyone else." I changed the subject again.

"Tell me about the average husband part," Colleen asked the next time she got a chance.

"Oh," I said, "not much of interest there, boring but nice, just average. But you will be well matched, do not worry. I am amazed that you have made such a determination at your age. You know exactly what you are doing and are happy with it." Once again I turned the conversation to her mother.

All during dinner Colleen kept interrupting to ask for more information about mediocrity. Six weeks later she had brought up her grades to As and Bs. She is now studying at one of the top universities in the United States and doing well in discovering the treasures of her brilliance.

THE COMFORTS OF THE MIDDLE

WHILE WE MAY admit that we are stuck, we usually are not aware that what we are stagnating in is our own mediocrity. We almost always prefer to observe our condition, not to berate and minimize ourselves with acknowledging the fact that we are responsible for it. Mediocrity is a term we prefer to use for other people, a way to demean them and maintain self-denial. The shock of recognition of our own mediocrity is the greatest motivation to change our course toward brilliance.

Unfortunately, mediocrity is something with which we are

all secretly familiar. Even if we do not use the word as descriptive of ourselves, we know when our life is not exciting and fulfilling. This common denominator should serve to keep us humble and compassionate of others' failings. Let us not forget that we are all in a process of growth and that we are at different levels in different areas. While some of us may have a fair number of aspects of our lives under control, that does not give any of us the moral authority to gaze in contempt at those living with mediocrity in the areas in which we have succeeded. Knowing that all of us have at least one mediocre area in our lives, not one of us is free to cast the first stone.

When people see mediocrity for what it is, few choose to remain in it, so let us now examine the full ramifications of this most contagious of character diseases.

MEDIOCRITY

WHENEVER WE MOVE away from our desire for brilliance in what we do and who we are, we move away from satisfaction. The key word is move. We are growing or deteriorating, doing more or doing less, learning or forgetting, falling or rising. Nothing stays the same. To be stuck is to stagnate. Stagnation leads to putrefaction. A stagnant situation is not an isolated professional, social or personal problem. It contaminates every aspect of our life and others' lives as well.

Sinking into mediocrity is a subtle process of safe and comfortable choices. The deterioration is insidious, eating up only little bits of us each day. It is so subtle that stagnating feels comfortable. The body is lazy by nature; the mind, capable of rationalizing anything; the will gets complacent. Though not particularly content, we are not unhappy either, so we must therefore be happy. And if we are happy, why change? The belief that doing nothing is easier than breaking our barriers of discomfort and uncertainty keeps us stagnant. By repeating the same acts, we continue to get the same results. These appear normal, giving us a false sense of safety and balance. In truth, as we move away from our potential for brilliance, we become less and less happy, which puts us on the road to depression.

We cannot see clearly in a state of stagnation because our critical faculties are infected. In the resulting confusion we unwittingly touch off a cycle of perilous events, one thing after another. Ineffectual efforts to get moving again create suffering. Sensing we are trapped and not knowing how to get out unleash negative emotions. The longer our stagnation lasts, the more we excuse it, which is a kind way of saying we lie. The more we lie, the farther away we move from our best intentions and dreams, farther from all that is life-giving to our spirit, to the truth of who we are meant to be.

Rather than brilliance, we seek what our dullness sees as comfort, which is to make minimum effort and to avoid discomfort. This makes us self-centered. Self-centeredness makes us inconsiderate. We lose respect for ourselves and others, and replace it with contempt. Burdened with failure, we feel no compassion for anyone's shortcomings, including our own. This negative attitude makes it easier and easier to be abrupt and disrespectful.

These start as small enough failings, but stagnation is a process. As our soul regresses, our service to others diminishes. We stop contributing to humanity; we damage others and become indifferent to the pain we have caused. This conduct is evil.

All about us suffer physical and moral contamination when one of us descends from his best self. What we have is what we give. As we abuse each other, we destroy our environment and the harmony of everyone around us. The blows inflict a cycle of anger, anxiety and pain. Eventually illness can erupt in the body because, unable to process so much brutality, we absorb it.

Most people have no language of hurt, instead they possess the language of rage—complaining, blaming, justifying themselves, swearing, screaming, insulting and defaming.

Mediocrity dulls our personality, isolates us from others, and depletes us of the brilliant energy that would be ours if we were not stagnant in our circumstances. It does not allow us to develop new qualities, skills or talents. These include strength of character, elegance of manner and the courage to open doors to new opportunities. We are existing, not living. We cannot be whole-hearted about anything, work, relationships or ideals.

Ironically, as we become discontented with our results, we demand immediate perfection. Having wasted so much time, we do not want to waste more in the effort of real improvement. If the current attempt to manifest our dreams is not perfect on the first try, we give up. In our confused state we do not see that we are repeating ourselves. We repeat by habit and surrender to habit.

The mediocre tend to transpose the very human need for satisfaction solely into acquiring wealth and/or winning a soul mate. There is nothing wrong with either pursuit, but as we become increasingly stagnant in fulfilling our potential for brilliance, the wealth is obtained at greater and greater cost to our humanity, and the so-called soul mate is won out of psychological neediness, not because we have inspired respect and love.

Marguerite, a student of mine, introduced me to Lawrence who inadvertently became an illustration of this sad dynamic. They had been sweethearts for two years and were engaged to be married in another two years when he finished medical school. A striking couple, I thought. He was tall, intelligent and charming. She was also tall and intelligent, and very beautiful. Both were very much in love.

Marguerite came from a loving, middle class family and had grown up with the support and encouragement that makes the United States a merit society. The future is not based on your past or who your parents are; it is based on working hard and persevering. The pitfall of being a self-made individual is that by lack of training you can remain rough of manner even when you reach the top. Marguerite, however, had inner strength wrapped in the grace of an educated lady.

Lawrence came from an old family that had lost its money, but he had absorbed a sophisticated manner as the result of being raised by refined and worldly parents. Lawrence seemed to have a certain toughness. He was also at ease with himself at any level of society and was able to put others at ease around him.

He spoke freely of his ambition to remake the wealth his family had enjoyed the generation before. After he and Marguerite got married, they would pay back his student loans and save what they could. The first investment would be to set up a private practice; the second would be to buy a house and start a family; the third, to begin a financial portfolio. Lawrence sighed. Those dreams looked so far away, but he was happy. He was more than half finished with medical school, was an excellent student, loved his choice of career and had a beautiful girl who would stand by him even when he had so much left to achieve.

Six weeks later Lawrence abruptly broke the engagement, saying that it was best for both of them. He was not going to be economically ready in two years, had nothing to offer

Marguerite and did not want to take more of her time. It depressed him, he said, having so little money that he couldn't take her out to restaurants and movies.

Marguerite was broken-hearted. When she could not convince Lawrence to change his mind because those things did not matter to her, she decided to move as far away as possible. It was inconceivable to her to live in the same city as Lawrence without running into him. She found and accepted a position as a research assistant with a company that had a branch in Europe. She went overseas. A few months after her departure, I received a letter from her.

In it she told me that Lawrence had married Sylvia, his wealthy cousin's ex-girlfriend. The cousin had been surprised in an indelicate situation with a married woman, a friend of the family, and had escaped to the Caribbean to wait for the storm to blow over. Sylvia, humiliated and despondent, was left to cry alone. Lawrence offered his shoulder. Sylvia was petite and pretty, not bright but sweet, and very, very wealthy, having inherited an enormous fortune a few years before. Apparently she was inconsolable. She cried and cried, and Lawrence was always at hand with his white linen handkerchief.

Consolation turned into a wedding. Lawrence and Sylvia moved to the East Coast where he transferred to an Ivy League university to complete his studies. The couple leased and decorated a beautiful apartment where they entertained graciously. (Marguerite knew this information because her mother had sent her social page clippings, and her friends had filled in the rest.)

Six years later Marguerite returned to the United States to visit family and friends. The years in Europe had served her well. She was wonderfully polished. If she was shining before, she was now an even brighter star.

Meanwhile Lawrence was established in a clinic in the best part of town. From mutual friends he heard that Marguerite was visiting. He called many times to ask Marguerite to meet him for lunch. At first she did not want to because she was afraid that seeing him again would take her back to the suffering of when they broke up. She told me later, "It took me a long time to recover and to get my peace back, but finally I went to meet him for lunch."

Lawrence was stunned by Marguerite's more mature beauty and her quiet elegance. And she thought he looked gorgeous in his designer suit.

"I've never forgotten you," he said. "I will always wish I was married to you."

Spellbound, Marguerite thought she was in love again, or rather, that she had never been out of love. Thank goodness, she told herself, that I'm going back to Europe in a couple of weeks!

They agreed to meet one more time. For dinner. "Just to talk," he said. When the date came, Marguerite looked more beautiful than she had a few days before, and he, she thought, now looked like a knight in shining armor. They talked about their lives during the past six years. Marguerite was excited by her accomplishments. She had overcome so much, learned two languages and absorbed another culture without losing her own.

Lawrence was entranced with admiration, but when his turn to share came, his manner changed. He seemed uncomfortable and kept information about his career to a minimum. He talked instead about what he had—house, boat, cars, membership at the country club—and the people he spent time with, an inventory of prominent names. It was obvious that there was no enthusiasm for his work or future. He had lost his love for medicine, his ambition, and with them his strong personality and dignity.

Marguerite found herself bored by his conversation. Friends offered other pieces of information with which she put together a more precise picture of Lawrence's life. Seduced by Sylvia's wealth, Lawrence had lost his incentive to work hard. He had not maintained his grades at the second university, so he returned to his West Coast alma mater where he managed to graduate but not with honors as would have been his old style. Sylvia then provided him with the clinic, but he had a limited number of patients, and colleagues did not consider him a serious physician. He and Sylvia had two children, but their marriage was not harmonious. Three years after the wedding Lawrence had an affair with an employee and was seen by too many people. Sweet Sylvia—betrayed, jealous and humiliated in a worse way than with the cousin—reacted violently and turned into a shrew. She checked up on Lawrence in every way she could; wanted to know his driving time, his phone calls, patients and duration of their visits, his every activity and any money he spent. They often argued in public. He was constantly humiliated.

Lawrence came to see Marguerite one more time. He said he loved her and wanted her back. He explained that he made very little money and he could not afford to support her. She would have to keep on working.

At first Marguerite believed he was proposing marriage, and she entertained the idea that she could help him breathe new life into his old aspirations. But then he made himself clear. He had not kept up on his reading; he was afraid to go off on his own. He could not afford a divorce now or ever. Marguerite would have to be his mistress.

Marguerite called me afterwards to tell me the end of the story. "I lost all respect for him. Funny. He stopped looking attractive to me. I guess because he's no longer the man I loved. I couldn't even be angry with him," she said, "because he's such a pitiful figure."

Lawrence believed that he could be nothing more than an average or below average doctor. He believed that he could fulfill his confused ideas of happiness if he had Marguerite with him. In spite of his high IQ and the advantages of a good education, he believed he was stuck in his career because he was irrevocably stuck in his marriage.

Because Lawrence had put so much of his life energy on acquiring quick wealth, he had won the soul mate he deserved. Although Sylvia surrounded him with all the things money could buy, they were both stuck in a life of misery in which they diminished each other constantly. Social status and prosperity gave him one kind of security, and Lawrence used them as his reasons for staying. For another man they would have been the glittering prizes of success. For Lawrence they had become the excuses of a coward.

Perhaps your unresolved situation is not so drastic, but once you have accepted staying stuck in it, you have accepted mediocrity as your existence. This built-in sabotage is your most faithful companion. During the day it is always present. It goes to sleep with you at night and is there waiting for you in the morning when you get up. The pursuit of happiness is a fantasy when one lives in mediocrity.

Brilliance
vs. Mediocrity

ALMOST EVERYONE WE know is stuck in some aspect or another. There is no shame in getting stuck. But it is shameful to stay there.

Living in brilliance and living in mediocrity are not compatible. One must be starved for the other to flourish. To eliminate mediocrity, we must know its habits, strengths and weaknesses. So far we have been discovering what we were meant to be, how we get stuck in what we are and why we allow stagnation. It was not one big decision that landed us in mediocrity, or an isolated careless one, but a sequence of small repetitive choices that stem from our present way of thinking.

To get out of mediocrity, we need to elevate our way of thinking. We need to know at what level our thoughts reside and how our thoughts at that level determine our actions. To adopt a new way of thinking, we must understand the three basic levels of thought—the superior, the mediocre and the inferior. Once we identify the level or levels in which we spend most of our time, we will be in a better position to elevate ourselves. We will from this point forward recognize the thoughts that drive us into mediocrity.

The Three Levels of Thought
SUPERIOR LEVEL

IMAGINE AN EAGLE or a condor or a hawk, one of the great soaring birds that seems motionless as it rides currents of air. In fact, its senses are constantly aware of the slightest change in pressure and direction. Eyes roaming landscape and clouds, it turns its head; there is a slight shift in flight feathers; it flaps its wings for a beat or two, and the bird dips and circles to continue to ride the sky. The gliding flight appears so graceful as to be effortless, but in fact the bird is always self-correcting.

Similarly, the individual in the superior level of thought lives in a state of constant self-correction. He takes advantage of his circumstances as opportunities to improve everything he is and all that he does; expands, learns, polishes and grows more and more elastic as he moves towards brilliance. His strength of character forbids him from being content with just copying and repeating his actions. Exercising his skills and virtues, he surpasses himself. A leader by merit, he inspires others to learn, improve, follow and support him in his contributions to the wider world. This thinker knows that he is the product of his choices and takes responsibility for them. He communicates his thoughts, feelings and intentions clearly and precisely.

The men and women on the superior level are leaders in all fields from arts and science to business and politics. These are fields of renown, but superior thinkers are also at work in gardens, homes and in factories. They filter their knowledge and wisdom to make life easier for those of us in lower levels of thought. Change and progress for all comes from their ideas. They create jobs for the rest of us and solve the problems of the disadvantaged. We owe them gratitude for they are responsible for the evolution of humanity in every aspect. When most people stop with riches and fame, those on the superior level often achieve greatness, honor and glory for their contributions. These individuals are very strong and move on with their beliefs even when the rest of the world is not in agreement. Always the fewest number of our society, their lives fill history. The Founding Fathers of the United States were such thinkers. So were martyrs like Joan of Arc and Socrates who were so committed to their truth that they chose to die rather than to live without it.

The efforts of superior thinkers to improve themselves and what they do place this group closer to perfection than the rest of us. It makes sense that their virtues include generosity and respectful consideration of others. We find elegant treatment in their presence because they understand dignity, theirs and ours. While compassionate to all human beings, they will not accept abuse if they can stop it.

The superior thinker is surrounded by the mediocre masses, and this makes his efforts toward perfection doubly difficult. The masses usually do not support anyone outside of the masses. The superior thinker would be fortunate if they could ignore him, but this is seldom the case. They will damage him if they can, mostly in covert ways because they are cowards.

Usually they defame his character. They go after his reputation because it is his most valuable possession. It does not matter that they derive no benefit from robbing him of it.

Conforming to the masses to be accepted is not a preoccupation for the thinker at the superior level. He accepts himself and the fact that his thinking is aligned with his values. His constant improvement brings clarity, and he uses it for his own benefit and for the benefit of others. He is conscientiously growing mentally and spiritually. He expands his own harmony continually, and that elevates his harmony with God. His attitude for living is that of gratitude. With this he nourishes and heals as much suffering as he can while he makes certain that he does not cause any.

Life is not easy at any level of thought. The masses may classify the superior thinker as weird, foolish or crazy especially when he is young. Yet he is a creator who brings change to the world which advances the masses. He may be envied and purposely dragged down. Loyal to his truth, he will not damage his attacker if he can avoid it, sometimes even to his own death, as was the case of Jesus.

Please do not let this picture discourage you from reaching for a brilliant and intelligent life. Few people in history have reached full potential, but it is making the reach that makes life worth living. It is in the reach that we meet our life's missions, our excellence, our happiness and our peace.

MEDIOCRE LEVEL

AS CHILDREN WE integrate into society by copying the examples of others—parents, teachers and so on. Most of us are satisfied with doing what we learn and doing it well. We are almost never concerned with improving it.

At the mediocre level of thought the individual repeats everything and changes little. All he wants is to get by and maintain his comfort zone, teaching his offspring the same mediocrity that he was raised with. When he does change, he does so slowly. Efficiency and excellence are not this individual's style. Adequacy is his norm, and resistance is his natural force. Resistance to change cements him in one place while he criticizes those who are growing. Resistant, he seeks to control others by preventing those above him from building and those below from destroying. History shows few records of success in controlling either group for very long.

Based on the quality of his choices, the mediocre thinker has an ambivalent opinion of himself. Mediocrity splits the human being into two different personalities: what we are and what we cover up. Masks, pretensions and personas are abundant and used to hide the truth. The mediocre thinker's confusion increases when he is not treated with the respect his pose is supposed to inspire.

While demanding responsibility from others, he takes none for who he is or what he does. Instead, he sees himself as a victim of his circumstances. He blames bad luck for what does not work but takes credit when things go well. When he has a new idea, it means he has taken it from someone else. The idea and the way he speaks about it, what he does with it and the results that follow are all diluted copies of the original.

Typically, no one stands out in mediocrity because there are no whole virtues there, only half virtues. Some mediocre thinkers are inclined toward good; others, toward evil. But there are no extremes among them. Many are good by default because they are not bad, and they are often described as nice. Qualities such as strength, inspiration, creativity, initiative, leadership, joy and elegance can never unfold at the mediocre level. Resistance to change causes mediocre thinkers to be bored and boring. Their lack of originality causes discontent and dependency. It foments envy and greed, fosters petty competition and covert violence, and sows the seeds of malice. Life in the mediocre level, a compromise of half-truth and half lie, is without dignity.

For the mediocre communication is reduced to an exchange of selective information. Their conversations are dominated by complaints, self-pity and gossip. In those inclined to malice, the conversation turns to greed, envy, bragging and defamation of character. Observe the biggest gossips and you will find people who are not doing much with their lives.

Ethics at the mediocre level are the same the world over. The mediocre approve, accept and support each other if it is convenient, and they deceive, betray and reject each other if it is convenient. They are incongruent by nature. The masses will accept that others have more as long as they consider them to share the same values. For example, the general public, even the poor, identifies with the wealthy characters of a soap opera as long as the characters are vulgar and immoral. "They are just like us," is the consensus.

While many of us choose to visit mediocrity, people who are truly average, unrepentantly vulgar and always conforming choose to live there. Mediocrity is the territory of the resigned masses.

At the mediocre level dreams of high caliber work and quality relationships always end in disappointment. The pervading resistance and weak ethics natural to this level are enough to contaminate the environment for those in their proximity.

Making mediocre choices may be comfortable and easy, but it makes life very complicated. Effort is continually wasted in compromises to keep the peace, to please others and to hide the truth. More energy is spent on covering up weaknesses than is necessary to grow out of them.

INFERIOR LEVEL

WHILE THE SUPERIOR thinker continually grows and the mediocre continually resists growth, the person embroiled in the inferior level of thought continually deteriorates. This individual subsists on society, sees no options for himself and does what he feels he must do in order to survive. Unlike the superior individual who creates or the mediocre who maintains, the inferior degrades, destroys and corrupts. He respects nothing and loves nothing for he knows nothing but fear and emptiness. Emotionally inadequate, he grew up unable to copy or imitate well enough to integrate into society. He nourishes himself from what he takes from others, especially their harmony. He is the conveyor of ruin. By nature he is ungrateful and enjoys nothing, neither what he receives nor what he takes. Love is a mere word to be used to entrap the unwary.

An extreme individual, he can be passive and aggressive, victim and victimizer, parasite and predator. As a parasite he manipulates and erodes. As predator he intimidates and attacks. Secretive by nature, he develops great discipline to cover his motives and actions. This individual hates himself and is mostly uncommunicative, but when he does speak, he expresses his frustration through lies, defamation or rage. His tale of woe, his excuses and the "evil" deeds of those that he sees as responsible for his situation are the main topics of his conversation whether he is in jail or on top of the world as a dictator.

The individual at the lowest level is devoid of virtues, possessing only nefarious tools developed through his hellish descent. Lying, manipulating, stealing and cheating are but a few of the tools. As a victim and as a parasite, he is destined to a life of leftovers. Only through misplaced pity does he receive whatever others are willing to give. He is used, disliked, feared, rejected or tolerated, but never accepted. He lives in constant fear for his life for as victim he is ready prey for another predator or hunted by the law.

The inferior level is the environment of deprivation and all that represents evil. The worst of human traits unfold at this level of thought, including all of the seven deadly sins—pride, covetousness, lust, envy, gluttony, anger and sloth. If the other levels do not succeed in controlling the inferior, its misfits will succeed in bringing society down altogether. The extreme in the inferior level make gruesome marks on history. It takes more effort to stand out as an evildoer than to stand out as a contributor to society.

IN WHICH LEVEL DO WE SPEND
MOST OF OUR TIME?

BE AWARE THAT there are many variations in each level and many nuances within the variations. Based on my best knowledge, I conclude the largest number of people live in the mediocre level. The second largest number inhabits the inferior. Together they represent approximately 80% of the population. That leaves 20% occupying the superior level, but a very small percentage resides there exclusively. Most of us reside in the mediocre level, slipping at times into the inferior and occasionally moving to the superior, oscillating between the two in a never ending struggle to maintain the middle ground.

The few who function mainly in the superior level occasionally fall out because of inferior choices. But no matter what our level of existence, all of us are capable of making superior choices. The option is always open to enter the superior level of thought and live a life of brilliance. It is never too early or too late.

The Three Levels of Thought

The thinker +	characteristic choices +	characteristic actions =	a life that is
SUPERIOR	wise	creative	independent
	courageous	inspiring	successful
	compassionate	freeing	happy
			abundant
MEDIOCRE	imitative	repetitive	dependent
	tentative	confused	dull
	self-serving	fearful	unhappy
			stagnating
INFERIOR	cunning	perverse	degrading
	predatory	malicious	violent
	selfish	confined	evil
			destructive

OUR MORAL AND MENTAL VEHICLES

I BELIEVE WE have two God-given gifts that allow us to make superior choices, and I will be referring to them from here on. They are at once distinct from each other and inter-dependent. We use them to move either toward brilliance or mediocrity, so I think of them as vehicles. They are critical for developing strength, and the way we drive them shows our purpose in life and determines the quality of our success. I call them moral and mental vehicles.

The word mental generally refers to the realm of the mind.

Actions are intimately connected with all thoughts whether we are conscious of the connections or not. Mental vehicle is my shorthand phrase for what we do. We do with our head and our hands, so to speak. In actual speaking we exercise intellect and vocal chords to do what is called conversation, so talking is part of the mental vehicle. More broadly, the mental vehicle is our work, the career or occupation we do for a living. We do not always get paid for what we do, so the term also refers to volunteer work, from a hobby to a charitable activity. "I am a writer" or "I am a mother and a homemaker" are specific descriptions of the mental vehicle.

While the mental vehicle is tangible and easy to identify as work or service, the moral vehicle is often invisible because it points to who we really are. The moral vehicle is an expression of our very essence, of our virtues or lack of them that are fundamental to our character and ethics. It represents how we do what we do. There are thoughts behind the moral vehicle of course, but I prefer to view them as coming from the spirit rather than the mind, hence the word moral. With the mental vehicle we can make a contribution to humanity, but it is the moral that determines the quality of what we give and the inspiration we offer.

My work teaches us how to use both vehicles intelligently and to keep them moving forward together. If one is more advanced than the other, we will experience imbalance first and desperation inevitably. A common example of this is the successful and vibrant executive who is known for his charm, charisma and creativity yet goes home to a dismal and loveless marriage. This man is in the end mediocre and will one day reflect on the "halfness" of his life.

Mental Vehicle	*Moral Vehicle*
WHAT WE DO	WHO WE ARE
Career	Spirit
Occupation	Habits
Service	Values
Intellect	Feelings
Skills	Virtues

We need to develop both moral and mental strengths to drive to brilliance. While we will never be perfect, we are getting closer. It is the quality of our journey that will make us shine.

BEGIN LIVING WITH COURAGE

WE CHOOSE THE level of thought we live in, and we can choose to leave it. If we are not where we believe we should be, where our lives are congruent with our soul, we need to stop and think. A ship at sea can change her landfall by a thousand miles with a mere two-degree shift in her present course. We too can radically affect the outcome of our lives with a few simple daily changes. A new course guarantees a different place of arrival, worlds away from the future we are building now.

But before we can take a step forward, we must identify our present ground as real. There are three requisites in doing so:

1. Accept ourselves for who we are now.
2. Accept that we are not who we are not.
3. Accept that we are responsible for the consequences of our choices.

The realization that we are living in mediocrity is painful, but to remain blind guarantees a lifetime of confusion and dullness. Identifying where we are stuck is the first step to getting out. From here we can take full control of our lives and with time put new order into our thoughts and conduct to unveil brilliance.

TWO QUESTIONS

WHENEVER I LECTURE on mediocrity, inevitably two questions come up at this point. Am I going to lose my friends and be left all alone if I get out of mediocrity? And what can I do about all the mediocre thinkers around me?

My answer to the first question is that you must distinguish between what is acceptable and what is not acceptable to you. You will not lose any friends because you improve yourself. But they might lose you if they do not treat you with the respect and consideration you are giving them. It is my experience that people of value, even when they are still stuck in mediocrity, do not wish to lose people of caliber from their lives. They upgrade their care of them, admire their efforts and appreciate their contributions to the friendship. Some friends who do not wish to grow and instead try to stop your growth eventually withdraw if you do not do so first.

At this very moment there are many people trying to surpass themselves, just as we are. We are going to meet some of them on the way to brilliance. There are also many that began to grow long before we did. They are waiting to mentor us and take us into their fold.

To the second question I recommend that you treat all people with dignity and compassion, in the same way that you would like to be treated by those above you. There are many who are living with less than we are, and I do not mean materially. Once again, we are human beings; we are not perfect and never will be; we all have weak areas that could use a lot of work. To think oneself better than others is arrogant, and arrogance is inherent to mediocrity.

A qualification of the above is this: if you have to put up with frequent envy and false accusations to be with people of different values, that is too high a price to pay for company. Do not accept disrespect from anyone. In general it is best to withdraw from any situation that diminishes you. Personally, I do not go where I know I am not appreciated.

CHAPTER 3

Making Distinctive Choices

The Forces behind Every Choice • How Moral and Mental Strength Work Together • Choosing with Conviction or Convenience • The Birth of Our Habits • How Strong Choices Eliminate Mediocrity • The Five Acts of Improvement

I WILL NEVER forget Rita. She faced daunting circumstances with limited material means, but what she did with her life proves the point of this chapter. For all practical purposes we are the products of our choices and control our own destiny. To be sure, biological and environmental factors have a great impact on us. These are our circumstances; what we do with them is our choice. When we are motivated by conviction as Rita was, we can energize our natural force of strength to move toward brilliance regardless of what may be obstructing us. Or we can give into the opposite force of weakness and sink deeper into mediocrity.

I was teaching in Mexico City when I came across Rita crying in a stairwell of the condominium complex where I was staying. She was the cleaning woman, hard working, and was well thought of by residents for whom she did many small favors. Gestures that to her were natural expressions of kindness were to all of us invaluable contributions to our busy lives.

Rita's problem, she tearfully told me, was that her husband had another woman. He demanded that Rita accept his lifestyle and never discuss it. He wanted peace at home, and all she had to do was accept the impotence of being trapped.

I invited Rita to join my class. The other students were ladies from prominent families, many of them married to men in the fashion industry. Their backgrounds were as advantaged as Rita's was impoverished, but their support and encouragement of her was genuine. Determined to grow, Rita became the star pupil who, because she had so little, inspired the others who had so much.

Whenever people struggle toward a common goal, bonds of affection grow quickly, and that was as true for my students as it was for me. With regret and anticipation we planned a graduation party that would crown our time together. It would be held in the beautiful home of one of the graduates. There would be a buffet; I would pass out diplomas for the course; and a few of the ladies would share their experiences with the more than seventy-five guests.

Rita declined to attend, admitting that she had nothing to wear for such an occasion. But her classmates could not imagine their graduation without Rita; they would not allow one of their own to fade away. One by one, the women offered Rita a designer dress, fine shoes, accessories, styled hair and makeup. Thus Rita was made ready for the party. After the brief ceremony Rita surprised everyone by standing up and requesting the microphone.

"Learning this education in the company of these ladies," she said in a soft and flowing voice, "has been like living in a dream. Until now I thought such fine ladies existed only in magazines, but they have received me as if I was one of their own and have treated me with a respect and sensitivity that were unknown to me.

"My people are poor. Perhaps the worst thing about being poor is ignorance. Ignorance makes you think that you have no choices. I went as far as third grade, higher than the rest of my family, but I thought that was as high as I could ever go. I want my children to go higher. I thought domestic work was the only kind available for a woman like me. Full of the illusions of youth, I moved in with a man when I was very young. I loved that man, and I thought he loved me too. I thought I had to accept his abuse as my lot in life. Everyone I know lives this way. I thought anger and indignity were part of loving a man. But to agree that it was his right to have another woman and to accept it as part of my life, I could not do.

"I never imagined I would be standing here with all these fine ladies that I feel so close to. But as you see, I am. I am trying to find words to say how thankful I am for being here and for what I learned. The gift of knowledge cannot be measured. My children share the good fortune of my new knowledge. Their lives are already different from mine, and my examples are their lessons. For the rest of my life I will speak up for my right to respect, and I will teach them about theirs. They will grow with a sense of dignity and without hate."

With a heartfelt thank you Rita finished her speech. There was a moment of silence then loud applause and many handkerchiefs drying tears.

On my last trip to Mexico Rita came to visit me. Her new

style of grooming made her look younger and prettier. Humiliation was in the past. Her husband kept begging her to come back, under any conditions that she wanted, but her love for him was also past. She made sure the children spent time with him, and they saw him more now than when they lived together. Rita's new self-confidence had attracted a new career. She now managed a beauty salon, no small feat of advancement for a domestic worker born with supposedly no options in a third world country.

No matter where we are born, we humans have the richest portion of all creation. We can choose to modify, adapt, create and give brilliance to ourselves and our world regardless of what may seem to be our limitations. We can choose to learn our lessons, move forward and leave suffering behind. We do not need to suffer to grow. We can choose either to use each day to push toward brilliance or to lose that day on our life's journey.

THE FORCES BEHIND EVERY CHOICE

AS APPLIED TO choices, I use the word strength specifically to mean the force for driving our moral and mental vehicles (who we are and what we do). Like developing a muscle, we build strength as we exercise existing talents and add new ones to exert ourselves beyond habit and complacency, pushing beyond what is familiar, comfortable and safe. Weakness is the antithesis. It is when we surrender to our indolence at what needs to be done. We either do nothing or do just the minimum to get by.

Behind the choices of strength and weakness are the corresponding motivations of conviction and convenience. Conviction is knowing what needs to be done. It leads to strong choices, creates a need to make more choices of strength and builds a pattern of self-confidence. Conviction is like a magnet toward brilliance, improving both our choices and the consequences that spring from those choices. What needs to be done sometimes seems difficult or strange because out of fear or laziness we have built a habit of weak and convenient choices, and detoured from our path of conviction.

Convenience is based on what is comfortable, immediately gratifying or easy. Choices of convenience drain strength and lead to choices that further weaken our moral and mental fiber. Convenience feels comfortable, and we generally avoid effort and discomfort, but the complacence leads to ruin. With convenience we yield to the force of weakness. We repeat what we do with the same habitual quality, deplete ourselves and are unable to improve the quality of the next act. To be content with what we already do well, without improving it one iota, is to give in to convenience. To procrastinate or to not even try to do anything is to cave in.

The following chart illustrates how the opposing forces of strength and weakness create opposite paths and opposite outcomes. There is a push and pull effect. On the path of strength we push toward our designed ideals. On the path of weakness mediocrity pulls us downward, and we resign ourselves to the darkness of our fate.

The levels of ascension and decline are represented as pyramids. The positive pyramid of strength and the negative pyramid of weakness are symbols for the strength and courage or weakness and cowardice we store as we succeed or fail. We naturally move from level to level, going up toward a breakthrough on one side, or going down to a crisis on the other.

On the conviction side we start each level needing a base of knowledge and skills, improve them and hone ourselves to a

Conviction and Convenience

**CONVICTION
(STRENGTH)**

FREEDOM

Hope and Faith
Destiny
Potential
Enthusiasm
Joy
Success
Self-esteem
Confidence

Breakthrough

Expectations   **CONVENIENCE**
Action   **MEDIOCRITY**   **(WEAKNESS)**

STAGNATION   No action
    Deterioration   Wishful thinking
    Weakness
    Crisis   Crisis
    Fear
    Self-doubt   Insecurity
    Self-dislike   Self-hate
    Discontent   Failure
    Limitation   Sadness
    Fate   Depression
    Unhappiness   Limitation
    Victimhood   Fate
                       Despair

                       VICTIMHOOD

peak of performance like an athlete preparing for a contest. When we complete the last necessary step of one level, we arrive at the threshold of the next opportunity. A breakthrough. With increasing strength we prepare for the next experience on our way to fulfilling our dreams.

HOW MORAL AND MENTAL STRENGTH
WORK TOGETHER

WE MAY BE intellectually prepared to move forward but not yet have the moral strength necessary for the opportunity we are seeking. All choices of conviction are acts of strength that affect all other aspects of our lives. We graduate to the next level only when our strength is complete. For example, we are not ready to start high school until we complete elementary school. Only then do we enter into the adventure of the next level of formal education. Our first day of high school is the first challenge at the new level. The concept that we grow to meet opportunity, rather than its coming to us, applies to any situation. What we have done before always builds the foundation for what will happen next.

Our present strength is never enough to win over a new challenge. We need to stretch from our comfort zone to surpass ourselves. We can easily solve problems that require equal or less strength than what we have now. To gain more strength, we must face a bigger challenge like the wrestler in the proverb who gains more strength by fighting a bigger wrestler.

The choices we make out of weakness are motivated by the convenience of what we feel like doing or not doing. Or if we are afraid or not. Accumulated choices of convenience build negative energy, the momentum that results from rolling backward and the natural stress that causes collapse. We descend to a crisis rather that ascend to a breakthrough. If we make a choice of convenience to fix a problem, we merely cover it and postpone a real solution. When we meet the problem again, and we will meet it again, we will be weaker and less prepared for the challenge. There are no solutions in convenience, only the worsening of circumstances and the guarantee that we will face another crisis.

We have learned about the false sense of stability known as mediocrity. Mediocrity occurs when the push of conviction and the pull of convenience supposedly balance each other. This creates a temporary place of stagnation identified by a subtle but constant deterioration.

Each of us is free to select and to follow any of our thousands of daily thoughts. We are free to live today by consciously doing what we know needs to be done with increased quality. We are just as free to live the day as if nothing, including ourselves, has much value, to keep doing things the same way we always have. We may think this is all right because no one will see or no one will know. But because we see and we know, we inadvertently treat ourselves as a nobody.

Please stop for a moment to do an exercise regarding your choices—past, present and future. From the unresolved situation we looked at in Chapter 1, write down:

- Two strong choices you could have made at the time of the situation but did not.
- Write down two weak choices you did make but would not make now.
- Write down two choices you wish to make in the future when your strength is greater than your problem.

I think this exercise will help to clarify your participation in the situation or problem. With new awareness you are free to make clear choices toward a solution.

CHOOSING WITH CONVICTION OR CONVENIENCE

EVERY CHOICE HAS consequences, and choices of strength give rise to at least three beneficial ones—high self-confidence, high self-reliance, and happiness in the experience of growth and forward movement. These will contribute greatly to new opportunities and higher caliber relationships in business, social and personal affairs. Another benefit, often uninvited, is the development of patience because good consequences sometime manifest subtly and may not be immediately apparent. If you recall the ship analogy, a slight shift in course will make the difference between San Francisco and Acapulco, but throughout the journey the ocean looks pretty much the same.

"Growing pains" is the phrase used to describe what attends the spurt from adolescence to puberty, when an adult's body grows around the child's mind and he has to accommodate strange physical changes along with the demands of more responsibility. Anything requiring stretching and growth from what was familiar causes some degree of pain or stress. Hence making changes of conviction and choosing strong actions initially feel uncomfortable. Different at least. But choices of strength lead us to greater peace of mind about who we are and greater expectancy about the opportunities ahead of us.

Improved language skill is a sign of making more choices based on conviction. As you grow into your new sense of satisfaction, you will catch yourself when you complain about a situation and use overworked phrases and cliches. Instead, the confidence of your conviction will make your language more precise and phrases like "Okay" and "Everything's fine" will no longer match your sense of well being and delight.

Another sign of growth is increased generosity. You will be less inclined to compete with or be envious of others. Self-satisfaction with weak choices is really a mask of convenience; it comes across as smugness that pushes people away. Authentic self-satisfaction accompanies conviction and opens the heart to act with kindness, to invite others in and to encourage them to grow.

Choices of weakness create a minimal quality of life. The consequences of weakness are all liabilities—disappointment, failure, humiliation, submission, rage, emptiness, self-destruction. Weakness pulls us further and further from the Ultimate Truth that reveals to us our unique truth. To the degree that we become despondent about the results of weak choices, there is less space left in our minds for accepting God's revelation of brilliance, so we do not have room for positive thoughts much less positive actions for getting there.

As human beings we are extremely gifted, so much so that using so little of what is available to us, we still manage to do quite a lot. Even with minimum effort we get by and avoid failure. Surely, we can achieve more exhilarating results by choosing to stretch just a little bit. Our untouched potential is waiting to be claimed. To ignore this opportunity is to ignore life.

THE BIRTH OF OUR HABITS

YOGIS IN INDIA say that it takes six weeks of repetition of the same action to create a habit and two years for the habit to evolve into a principle, a pillar of inner truth that manifests our character. Western experts in behavioral modification have slightly different time frames, but they essentially agree. To continue our journey to brilliance, we need to get into the habit of stretching from weak choices to strong ones. The question is, How?

We choose to.

Our next step is always evident. But if we do not feel like it or are afraid, then we cannot see what to do. There are no shortcuts to brilliance. It is crucial to accept what needs to be done and to choose to do it. Doing it now improves who we are and our circumstances. Seeing them more clearly, we create new solutions to our old problems and build the strength to implement the solutions and leave the problems behind. An inspirational example involved a student of mine named James.

In our first conversation James described how he felt about his job as an elevator salesman. He hated the equipment and loathed the clients. He disliked the office out of which he worked, its location and everything in the vicinity, from bathrooms to vending machines. He despised the management staff and his co-workers. It was hard to pinpoint what James hated most. In a tie for special disdain were having to punch in and out on a time clock and mandatory attendance at motivational meetings.

Desperate to get out of his situation, James was receptive to my idea of using his job as a springboard to develop the qualities that would elevate him to the next level of opportunity. He purposefully diverted his energy from hating everything to acting respectful regardless. His homework was to be professional with his clients, no first names unless invited to be familiar and no intrusive remarks or jokes. I reminded him to keep his word and to be efficient. He was to be punctual, and to appear clean and groomed. Last but not least, he had to show respect for his resources and management, i.e. colleagues, supplies and office equipment. He was to develop a respectful style as a way of being.

James' choosing to be more efficient led to two extra sales calls a day, and they brought extra commissions. Soon James was so busy creating more business, he had to arrive at the office two hours before everyone else and sometimes left several hours after closing. Being in the field so much excused him from attending the meetings that he despised. He broke sales records. Management told him to throw away his punch card and to come and go as he saw fit. James seized the opportunity and turned his five-day workweek into four, which he had previously thought would be impossible.

Performance begot performance. James' income continued to climb, but now he had time to pursue recreational activities that had alluded him. The quality of his relationship with his girlfriend improved from worrying about not spending time with her to enjoying her company.

Months after our work together was over, James called me from San Francisco. His company was flying him all over the United States so that he could share the secrets of his success. His fantasy of telling management off had become reality, and he was getting paid for it! The last I heard about James came in the form of a company newsletter in which he was acclaimed the number one salesperson of the year.

Any situation in life is a good place to apply our new knowledge and to exercise the choices of strength. With a fresh perspective we can improve all of our circumstances and see challenges as necessary lessons for excellence.

HOW STRONG CHOICES ELIMINATE MEDIOCRITY

IT IS NOT necessary to enter into a great battle to begin improvement. We do not have to do anything radical or unnatural. We do not have to concentrate all of our present strength for one isolated moment to force out that troubling situation we spend so much time worrying about. Just as simple small choices got us to where we are, slight improvements will allow us to develop the clarity and the strength to resolve the situation. By not nourishing our weakness, we will allow it to starve to death.

As we upgrade the quality of small choices, we soon leave mediocrity behind. If we do not like the result of our accumulated choices, we need to change our way of thinking. Any improvement is born from a clear thought. Even a small improvement denotes effort, and effort generates energy. A series of small efforts toward a goal energizes our courage, raises our self-respect and reinforces our conviction that we are creating a pyramid of strength.

THE FIVE ACTS OF IMPROVEMENT

SO LET US begin building strength by doing what I call the "Five Acts of Improvement" everyday. This is a very simple exercise, almost deceptively so, that will become fundamental to changing your life in thousands of profound ways. As you learn more, you will see how the acts have multiple applications to every area of your life. In time you will discover more acts that you choose to do because they invigorate your whole life.

Think of five things you do that you can improve or five things that you should be doing that you do not do at all. Choose simple things like making the bed, straightening up your desk or pushing in a chair when you are done with it.

These choices of strength, motivated by conviction, will mold the thinking you will need to move up to new opportunities.

1. *Do what needs to be done throughout the day.*

We know what they are, all those little nagging things that should be done today. Doing them badly is better than not doing them at all. We can always improve them as we go along.

2. *Stop blaming, complaining or justifying yourself.*

We know when we have not done what needed to be done or if the quality we offered was less than adequate. Justifying our behavior is acting as a victim. If we realize that most of our problems are the result of leaving things undone, we will become more alert to do them when they need to be done.

3. *Elevate your language.*

The Latin word for masses is *vulgo*. Vulgarity is the English word for the language of the masses. We know when we are not using correct language to express ourselves. Describing precisely what we feel is more satisfying than using the vague, abrasive or vulgar language of mediocrity.

4. *Be more compassionate.*

We know when we are competing, showing off, putting others down or gossiping or talking about things they do not want to hear. This is the opposite of compassion and not only cements us in mediocrity but also sinks us into malice. We reveal loud and clear our low quality of being.

5. *Do not surrender to the resistance we already have within ourselves.*

Of course it is hard, but we can try and keep trying. We want to get out. Are we are afraid of going forward, or are we afraid of giving up? It is much easier to live with the fear of what we are going to meet if we go forward because we already know the misery of going backward.

I am sometimes accused of giving kindergarten homework to adults, but the goal of the Five Acts of Improvement is to train the mind to develop the attitude of constant self-correction, which is the first attribute of a superior thinker. The exercises above are not about making the bed; they are about establishing a way of thought that guarantees continuing growth. We can all do a spectacular deed or two, but they will not change the pattern of our thinking. Small steps establish a habit of conviction that becomes a way of life. From that will flow brilliance, not in isolated events, but as a strong reflection of who we are. We can reach this elevated level in simple steps that are relatively effortless. Or we can view the steps as trivial, do them hit and miss, and stay exactly where we are until gravity takes over.

Each of us has an important mission in life, but until we exercise strength of character, we will not be prepared to fulfill it. A student of mine named Jeffrey grew up in a ghetto where there were no opportunities to go to college except by earning a scholarship. He applied himself in academics and in sports, and won an athletic scholarship to a prestigious university. From there he went on to a career in professional athletics. Sensitive to the people who were part of his humble beginnings, Jeffrey frequently went back to visit his old neighborhood. He did not try to overtly influence the young people there, but he helped where he could. His presence was so brilliant, he really did not have to say anything. Tell Jeffrey or those he inspired that simple arithmetic or learning the basics of throwing and catching a ball or the fundamentals of sharing are meaningless homework. Jeffrey's example provided the fuel for dozens of boys and girls to aspire to and attend college.

Our small choices influence the way we feel about ourselves, which in turn influence our behavior. Our behavior affects others. The effect of all of our choices as a society is what characterizes a nation. Each one of us is free to make a contribution or to detract from the common good. Each nation affects the whole world. And it all begins with one person making a single choice.

The Dance *of* Life

AFTER SEVERAL YEARS of living in the United States as a teen-ager, I yearned for the taste of life in my native country. I wanted to continue my studies in El Salvador, and my father was not happy about it. He agreed, however, on one condition—that I would go to boarding school—and I accepted. The next three years were a very happy time for me.

Instituto Bethania is a Catholic school in the European style. The entire student body is never more than 125 girls, and the waiting list to register is enormous. The discipline of the school is refined; everyone is treated with respect; and the beautiful culture is jealously maintained.

Even though the school was expensive and exclusive, it had no household help except in the kitchen. We girls had to clean every other room that we used—bathrooms, bedrooms, sitting rooms and classrooms—and every hallway we trafficked. The chores were rotated every week so that each of us could learn how to clean every room. Our chores were always inspected and gently evaluated by a sister.

In my first week I was assigned the main corridor, a ceramic tile space of approximately 20 by 80 feet, half opened to the grounds with a low wall and arches. I completed my chore and put the mop away. While I was waiting for inspection, the Mother Superior, Sor Maria de la Cruz, walked by. She was a very strong woman, easily the strongest I have ever known, strict and consistent, but ever so gentle at the same time. "Who is responsible for this corridor?" she asked.

"I am, Mother," I proudly answered.

"Come here," she said. "Look at the floor and tell me what you see."

I was sixteen years old, loving my life and very romantic. I promptly began, "I see the reflection of the sky, clouds and the foliage of the trees. . . . "

"Look again."

Silence.

She did the talking. "If you look at the floor carefully you will see several dozen streaks you have made with your mop. There is an eight-streak maximum. You will have to do it again."

"Yes, Mother," I said. So I did it again. And again. Four more times that day. The eight-streak maximum was hard to meet, but I did it.

The next day I had to mop only three times to get within my quota, and I did better the day after. The fourth day I became very attentive so I could discover the action that created the streaks. I saw that it happened when my arm got tired and I dropped the mop or stopped.

I was taking flamenco classes on the weekends, and I was very conscious of the constant movement of the dance. I tried to apply the same sense of rhythm to my mopping. I did not drop the mop or pause the whole time. I glided backwards across the floor making figure eight's with my mop until the entire floor was complete. I checked my work. There were no streaks.

"How did you do it?" asked Mother Superior. "It is perfect."

I showed her my flamenco-style mopping method.

"This has never happened before! You have taken this to mastery! From now on," she declared, "you are the Master Mopper. I now give you the responsibility to teach this to all the other girls. They will train the new ones next year. There will never again be streaks on this floor."

I was so proud and so happy, the Master Mopper! When my father came to pick me up for the weekend I told him the story. He chuckled. Then he grew serious. "My little daughter, you have discovered the ballet of life. Whenever you see someone doing what he or she does efficiently, and it looks easy and graceful, remember that you are in the presence of a master. If we all did this, life would be as gentle as the petal of a rose."

This was a pivotal moment in my life. The exhilaration of taking something to mastery awoke in me a great hunger to experience it over and over again everywhere I could. I did not know then that mastery was brilliance, but the appetite to taste it again opened a new and secret world for me, that of taking my responsibility to the highest point I could reach. On the way I discovered the biggest treasure yet, the greatest feeling, the most tender of human experiences. It is the gratitude for being.

CARE AND APPRECIATION

SIMPLY PUT, RESPONSIBILITY is taking care of someone or something. Caring means to cherish, to hold something dear enough to maintain it in good condition, and to upgrade it and add value whenever possible. In this we gain respect for what we are taking care of. We learn from it. As our appreciation of it increases, we grow in appreciation for ourselves. The full benefits of caring come when the mental vehicle of our work and service is in harmony with the moral vehicle of who we are. Then responsibility encompasses our minds, our bodies, our well being and our planet. Our caring embraces everything in our environment—others, our possessions and theirs, ourselves, our talents and gifts, and theirs too. Thus responsibility becomes a profound expression of thanksgiving for all the good things that we are, have and do.

Every strength of character and grace is born from the effort of giving care. Discipline, courage, initiative, organizational ability and mental acuity name only a few of responsibility's many children. Because our moral and mental vehicles cover all aspects of our lives, it follows that managing both responsibly leaves nothing important neglected. We will do what we do well and get better at it. We will try new things and get better at them. We will sharpen awareness of our principles and refine them. We will embrace higher values and grow in virtue.

It is natural to take care of what we love, but in some cases we may not even like what we have to take care of. The commitment of responsibility is to do our best regardless. Then if nothing else, we will appreciate the value of what we give and improve the quality of who we are. We will come to more deeply cherish the good things in our lives.

Among the good things that need to be taken care of are self-respect and self-love. They are consequences of satisfaction and joy, which are two more of the offspring that living with responsibility produces. The knowledge that we are improving who we are and what we are doing creates and adds to self-esteem. When we take care of others, we encourage and nourish them, but we cannot give them self-esteem. It is an intimate outpouring of how we manage our own two vehicles.

Some people attribute luck as the reason that others have talents, gifts, good friends, a loving family, fulfilling work, invitations to nice places, property, health, beauty, you name it. But the good things in our lives are not matters of luck. If we do not care for them, we will lose them. They are enormous responsibilities. Luck is the word the lazy use to justify the success of the responsible.

Most people view responsibility as an obligation, a duty and a burden. They do not see it as the wonderful opportunity it is and so fail to take advantage of it. Anything that demands attention and care is our path to the next level of growth, where higher opportunities await us. An opening, should we seize it, will take us to a deeper discovery of who we are, what we can grow to be and how to experience the fullness of life right now.

To view responsibility as hardship shuts us off from the immediate opportunities all about us. If we do not take care of what we have in our lives now, we lose the opportunity to take care of more things in the future. We can take care of only the opportunities that we are equipped to take care of. What purpose would it serve to attract an opportunity that we cannot handle? (Except of course as a good reminder that we need to develop more qualities to reach it.) The new challenge is never bigger than we are but is bigger than our strength at the moment. When we want greater opportunities than the ones we have, we must increase our acts of responsibility to build up the strength necessary to meet the new challenge.

Whether we are aware of it or not, our behavior is constantly monitored by others, and herein is where most of our opportunities stem. Word of mouth is still the greatest marketing tool; our reputation is our best product.

To be responsible in the way we care for the best of who we are, we need to understand the virtues, values, qualities and skills that make up our strengths. We can recognize skills, such as organizational ability and manual dexterity, and identify qualities like punctuality, being cooperative and having a warm personality, but values and virtues are subtler to distinguish. Strictly speaking, a value is related to culture and tradition, and its merit may be relative, whereas a virtue is universal and timeless. The words are so often used interchangeably, we need to understand only that they are rooted in our moral aspect. They are all the good things that emanate therefrom, like honesty and kindness, compassion and courage, love and generosity. It is important to understand that these are not isolated strengths. They exist in clusters. For example, where there is gratitude there is kindness, gentleness, appreciation and love.

Character flaws also exist in clusters. They are connected to values in that they are their extreme opposites. Order is the opposite of disorder; generosity, the opposite of selfishness; love, the opposite of hate; and so on. We are either pushing toward a value or slipping toward a flaw. The cluster factor means that it is not just one thing that will add strength or take it away. If we take responsibility with one virtue, we are also exercising those associated with it.

THE LAW OF RESPONSIBILITY

THE ADAGE THAT the teacher learns as much from his students as they do from him is pretty accurate. I had a two-hour session with a gentleman who was in despair because no matter how hard he worked he made only enough money to survive. "If you can tell me what I'm doing wrong, I will figure out how to fix it," he said. "Right now I don't know what it is that is causing my failure, but it has been going on for the last ten years. I'm at the end of my rope."

I am not being generous with the word when I call him a gentleman. He was truly a good man—honest, well mannered, and a very hard worker. He was highly educated and expressed himself clearly. Tall and handsome, he dressed the part of a gentleman. But he was a failure. A gentleman failure.

The expression on his face betrayed his depression. I asked him what he did for a living. "I'm a businessman," he told me. "I find products, make sure that they are well made, design a beautiful package and create a marketing program. But no matter what I do, I never do more than break even. What's wrong?"

I asked him to describe a few of the products he marketed. As he did so, I began to see a pattern. None of his products had any moral value for his consumers. His last project was marketing an expensive video on gambling. I asked him to ignore the material value of the products and to evaluate their moral value on a scale of one to five, five being the highest point. He thought for a moment and looked at me with wonder.

"Three at best," he said.

"That is the problem," I replied. "Your product is expensive, and your effort is excellent, but the value of what you are selling is mediocre at best." To relieve him of a bit of the pain at his own waste, I told him the story of a seamstress I knew.

Her work was exquisite, *haute couture.* She could copy anything, and working from instructions her clients gave her was how she made a living. Her finished product could be examined on the inside, and you would find perfection, not a single raw edge. On her own she designed and made some garments that were of equal workmanship but never sold, and she could not understand. They were the most beautifully made ugly clothes that I had ever seen!

Out of the first meeting with the businessman I discovered a general principle that puts the incidents together. My contention to him was that he would enjoy better income if he raised the moral quality of his choices to the high level of his hard work. My hypothesis about the seamstress was that her designs would sell if her choices reflected as fine a sense of taste as the meticulous quality of her work. What I call The Law of Responsibility suddenly revealed itself.

There has to be an alignment between the quality of our choice, including the motivation behind it, and the effort we put into getting the result we want. If the quality is less in one of these areas, we will not have the desired result no matter how much quality there is in the others. The Law of Responsibility can be summarized as a formula for clear thinking. Its variables are applicable to almost every aspect of life.

Choice + Responsibility = Result

1. Conviction	+	100% (full effort or care)	=	Great success
2. Conviction	+	50% (mediocre effort)	=	Mediocrity
3. Convenience	+	100% (full effort)	=	Mediocrity
4. Convenience	+	50% (mediocre effort)	=	Failure

The first variable of the formula gives you the only guarantee of success. If all your elements are top quality and you still do not get the expected result, you more than likely need more information than you have, and a consultation with someone who knows more than you in this area is called for.

The new fact or idea may be a simple adjustment to how you look at the problem. Even if no one has a clue, trial and error provide their own enlightenment. Thomas Edison and many others have pointed out that the failures of invention, discovery and "impossible" achievement help narrow focus on what can work. Thus the errors are building blocks to eventual success.

Variables two, three and four of The Law of Responsibility show the basic incongruity of offering the minimum and demanding the maximum in return. Living with minimum or no responsibility confuses us to opportunities that are available. Unaware or dishonest with what we offer, we pray for better and more opportunities, and are answered with challenges to develop the strengths necessary to build from what we know. But our incongruity rejects the opportunity to grow.

Most people live in the effects of variables two and three, the shaded area. To illustrate how The Law of Responsibility applies to them, let us evaluate two different situations, one in business and one in a relationship.

A good company with a good product but inefficient management will misuse an excellent worker by degrading his output, mistreating him or diminishing his love for his work. The employee is then rendered mediocre when in essence he is efficient. The company will automatically lose money on this employee because he will not produce what he is capable of. I know of companies that hire creative people and then fight their every idea and project. It is not unusual either that when a creative person wins the fight and the project is recognized with awards, those who fought against it will take the credit. The pattern will repeat itself until they wear out the creator and crush him until he quits. Then the company hires another and starts the same game all over again.

In a marriage or a love relationship consider a couple in pain because of their differences. One is responsible, utilizes conviction in both moral and mental vehicles, and gives quality care to every aspect of the relationship. The other may be successful in a career but is not considerate in many areas, including the relationship. This would put the couple in variables two and three. As The Law of Responsibility would indicate, one person cannot create harmony for two; at best you will have a mediocre relationship. Individuals in troubled relationships often ask me if people change. The answer is yes for those who want to grow. They improve until they become brilliant human beings, but most people do not want to make the required effort.

Blinded by love, naiveté, wishful thinking, fraudulent representations or lack of self-knowledge, many people make erroneous choices. A high caliber person married to a partner who lives in mediocrity has no hope for anything other than a mediocre marriage unless the other partner wants to raise the level of his responsibility for the relationship. For the high quality spouse, the mediocre partner is usually resistant to change, wants to control the spouse and will do whatever he can to stop the spouse's growth. It is not to the benefit of the mediocre to have a shining partner because the contrast makes dullness so evident.

Angela was an ambitious career woman who met and married a good man who accepted her with her aspirations. Charles adored her. Angela was happy. They planned their lives and agreed on the main issues. They wanted to start their family right away, have two children or three if they did not have one of each gender, and when the children were in school, Angela would go back to her career.

Their plan came into being as they had foreseen it. Charles formed his own company. They bought a house, and reared a boy and a girl to school age. By then they could afford two cars and a part time housekeeper. Angela prepared to go back to her career. That is when the plan began to unravel.

Charles was furious. He did not want his wife to work. After a year of many arguments they compromised. Angela would work from home, freelancing on a part time basis.

Angela was good at writing advertising copy, and she presented herself in an engaging manner, so her career flourished in spite of the limitations. Charles began sabotaging her work, verbally destroying what she put together to the point of demeaning her abilities in front of her clients. As time went on, he made cutting remarks about her personality, interrupted her in front of friends and finished every story she began to tell. Angela tried the usual avenues to save her marriage. Charles was nominally supportive, but he continued to put her down and to demand that she give up her career to dedicate herself to being a wife, mother and homemaker. Angela would not give up freelancing, but the emotional abuse became so intense that she almost lost her love for her work.

When the children were old enough to help care for themselves, Angela asked for a divorce. Charles was devastated. He said he loved her and that he was happy. She could not understand how he could be so happy when he made her so miserable. Years after their divorce when their emotions calmed down, Angela asked him why he would not let her work in her career, especially when he had supported her in her ambitions when they decided to get married. "Because," he answered, "I was afraid that if you were successful you would leave me."

"And why did you put me down?" she asked.

"I didn't mean to," he said, "I just wanted to stand out, and I couldn't when you were present."

WHEN VALUES FALL INTO WEAKNESS

IT IS MUCH easier to apply responsibility to our mental vehicle because the areas are visible and tangible. We all can improve what we do and take care of what we have, and the next step to do so is always evident. Not so with our moral vehicle because virtues are intangible. Most of us take our virtues for granted and think of them as normal, instead of realizing them for the special gifts they are. To improve them we must exercise them.

The most difficult application of the Law of Responsibility is to ourselves. Allowing people to manipulate us into giving what we do not wish to give is being irresponsible to who we are. It is perfectly acceptable to decline giving away your money, your time, your work and even your love by politely stating your choice. There is no need to defend conviction.

"I'm generous but people take advantage of my generosity," is a common complaint. The value of generosity emanates from gratitude, the deepest desire of the soul to reflect the brilliance of God's love. Generosity is an absolute virtue, and in the superior level of thought it is a great strength that cannot be exploited. What is taken advantage of is our weakness. When our generosity falls into weakness, we are vulnerable to exploitation.

When our virtues fall into weakness they lose their names. Admiration, affection, loyalty, friendship, trust and love are all hard won. To dispense them without responsibility degrades their value. It assumes a worthiness in the recipient that is based on our false expectations, or what we wish rather than what we know to be true, which take time and effort to discover. We assume what we want to see, and set ourselves up for disappointment, humiliation and betrayal. Seeing ourselves as victims means we are rejecting our responsibility toward ourselves. People treat us the way we allow them to.

The following chart illustrates values we too often degrade and thus allow to fall into weakness.

VALUE	WEAKNESS
"I am too . . . "	"People take advantage of me because..."
Honest	I divulge too much personal information.
	I give uninvited opinions.
Generous	I am easily manipulated into giving more than I want to.
	I give to gain benefit.
Hospitable	I say nothing when people intrude.
	I allow myself to be taken for granted.
Friendly	I am so eager to please others that people walk all over me.
	I give friendship before it is earned.
	I become familiar.
Trusting	I give trust before it is earned.
	I expect everyone to trust me.
Pleasant	I allow people to break my harmony.
	I pretend that I am not offended.

Using our moral vehicle irresponsibly opens the door to predators who will take advantage of our weakness. The reason is simple: that is what predators do. Our best protection is to be responsible for what we give.

Honesty goes hand in hand with the responsible use of our moral vehicle, and dishonesty is the constant companion of irresponsibility. Accepting love, friendship or opportunity that we know we cannot take care of with quality is basically dishonest. Accepting them under the pretense that we will be responsible when our habits are mediocre is fraud. To give them without a thought to irresponsible persons is just plain foolish.

LIFE WITH MINIMAL RESPONSIBILITY

ONE EVENING A social acquaintance of mine who lives in another state called me from the airport. Susan said that she was in Los Angeles on business and that a friend who was to pick her up and let her stay in her home was nowhere to be found. In El Salvador people customarily extend themselves in emergencies, so I opened my home to Susan until the friend turned up, but I said I could offer neither time nor transportation.

"No problem," she said.

The next morning Susan approached me for a ride to her first appointment. I said I could not oblige. She asked to use my car. I said that my car was my transportation. Susan made several telephone calls, found someone with a car and spare time, and even tracked down the friend who no longer wanted Susan in her home. Susan asked me if she could extend her stay with me to a week. I said yes and reiterated my original offer: my hospitality still did not include time and transportation.

"No problem," she said.

By nightfall of that first day Susan had gone through all of my drawers and cupboards. She knew where everything was and helped herself to personal items. The week of her stay stretched every couple of days and became three weeks. Susan loved lounging in a hot bath for hours, never once troubling herself with the thought that students and friends might want to use my home's single bathroom. I once found her reading what I had written on my computer that day and stood watching her for several minutes until she finished, whereupon I asked her opinion. I have to give Susan some credit for having some sense of shame. Although she flatly denied having read anything, she did blush.

Susan's lack of consideration was a direct result of her being irresponsible. Irresponsible people are naturally selfish. I too was irresponsible in regard to my things and the intrusions of a boorish guest, but I kept thinking that the next day was going to be Susan's last. When her last day finally did dawn, I actually refrained from jumping and cheering.

Susan had several appointments that day, two on the far side of the city and one nearby, and she asked me to drive her to all three then to the airport. That would have taken six hours out of my work, and I said no. Susan cancelled her first two appointments and arranged to meet an airport shuttle at the office building where her third was to be held, but she had difficulty getting a taxi that would take her to that appointment on time. I calculated I could probably drop her off and return home to prepare for a conference that was an hour and a half away.

It was twenty minutes to the office building with several more circling the block until Susan could figure out where the correct entrance was. While she ran into the building, I began unloading her luggage onto the sidewalk. She dashed back to say that she would take only ten minutes. I should wait then drive her and her luggage around the block where she was to meet the shuttle. "That possibility does not exist," I said, and I finished taking her things out of the trunk of my car.

"I know what your schedule is!" Susan shot back in a shrill voice. "You've got enough time to wait for me and take me to the other side. You'll still get to your meeting on time."

I did not grow up with shouting, so I have an automatic switch. "Do not raise your voice at me," I said. Susan's voice jumped nearly two octaves higher, and she began screaming at me like an irate vegetable vendor in a village market in Latin America. Perhaps under different circumstances I might have had a nostalgic pang for my homeland. Instead, I called Susan ungrateful and left her on the curb, yelling at my retreating car.

After I got home, she telephoned from the airport to tell me very calmly that she had been right. Her appointment had lasted only ten minutes and I could have waited for her and driven her and her luggage to the other entrance. I started to say— But but her screams cut in, so I hung up.

After she landed she called yelling, "You're supposed to know etiquette! How dare you hang up on me! Who do you think you are?"

"I do not think, I *know* who I am," I said.

"Don't you dare hang up on me again!"

"It is unintelligent to listen to insults and violence," I said, "and intelligence precedes etiquette." Click. Several calls followed. I did not pick up the telephone. When I checked my voicemail, there were several screaming messages that I erased without listening to. But I wrote Susan a letter stating that I could not be in any relationship in which I had to fight for each of my personal rights and therefore was withdrawing my friendship. The last I heard from Susan was on my answering machine. "It is difficult to be your friend," she declared.

Although I demonstrated the virtue of hospitality by inviting Susan into my home, it was weakness to ignore her intrusions for so long, to the point that she believed they were her rights. Comment does not have to be made at the moment of transgression, but unless it is made at some point, we are not helping the other party. I was at a disadvantage because I never knew that she meant to stay three weeks. In any case, I should have spoken after the first transgression. I am certain Susan did not mean to harm me personally. She was living her habits, and I had every right to reject them and clarify my position. Most people blunder socially more out of ignorance and insensitivity than from malice, but we have the right to withdraw from situations that are damaging to us.

It is fascinating to note that most people live in mediocrity and consequently are reactionary versus action taking; yet most of us do not react with gratitude. We do not bother with the simplest of "thank-you"s. It is when things are not to our liking that we react. We react with displeasure or rejection.

In the give and take of human affairs reactions are congruent to the actions we take or do not take. The knowledge that for every action there is a reaction is a valuable, scientific fact. The choices that we make will create certain consequences that we can expect, positive or negative. We can then take responsibility for the reactions we create. If the reaction is not what we expected, we have the right to ask if there is anything we did or said to merit that response. If we are blameless, the person will usually pull back and apologize. If we are not, we must be prepared to hear of the damage we have caused and rectify it. Justified criticism is useful to fine tune our ideas and improve our performance. Destructive criticism, on the other hand, has no value.

There are evil people who do wicked things to others who have not merited the attacks. If you see rage as a reaction, withdraw. Rage is emotional, unreasonable, uncontrollable and dangerous. People in a rage are not interested in solving the situation, only in venting their wrath.

Each of us is unique and has a distinct purpose that fits beautifully into the design of the universe. This is as true for a king as it is for a day laborer, and the best design for either one is to live with full responsibility. What makes us special is fulfilling our purpose and making a contribution to others. Our specialness is measured in the quality of our service and our conduct in all relationships. We are responsible for our potential and can reach it only through the contribution of our work or service and through being who we are. It is not possible to improve everything, but we are always in a position to improve something within our immediate thoughts and deeds.

It is far easier to live with our consequences when we have been responsible, rather than to live with the consequences of irresponsibility, which will always be more difficult and depressing. When we accept responsibility for what we do and who we are, something magical happens.

We change.

We begin to shine.

The desire for the full happiness promised by The Law of Responsibility never goes away. In the last part of life when youth is left behind and our most productive years are a memory, we all take inventory of our lives. Let it not be from anger and bitterness of the opportunities not taken, but rather from the peace of knowing that we have used our years honorably by being responsible.

No matter where we are, this is not a time to mourn for the years wasted. This is the time to change through acts of responsibility and to begin our new life of brilliance.

Take a moment and think of what responsibility means in your family, relationships, work, health or spiritual development. How do you take care of those you love or say you love? How do you show appreciation for those who have contributed to you? Do you recognize their values and give credit where credit is due? Do you care for contributors by thanking them, or do you secretly resent them?

1. Add a little extra effort to your five daily acts of improvement.
2. Express appreciation even if you do it intimately to yourself.
3. Verbalize the values of others when the opportunity offers itself.

CHAPTER 5

How Are You Remembered?

An Authentic Impression • The Importance of a Pleasant Expression • The Significance of Every Encounter • How To Be Forgotten • For Every Choice There Is a Rejection • How To Be Interesting • The Burden of Pretension • The Dangers of False Images • The Unforgettable Impression • We Are All that We Do • Projecting a Better Image

WE ALL WANT to make a good impression wherever we go. Striving toward brilliance, we should want even more to make an unforgettable and beautiful impression. This is not for ego's sake. Rather, it is for the benefits of our contribution and the inspiration our values may offer others.

It is through the impressions we make that people accept us, reject us, ignore us or, worse, just tolerate us. Toleration is sufferance and feels humiliating. We seldom mistake its presence. It is as if people were saying to us, "You are here; we know it. We wish you weren't, but we'll put up with you." It is also very clear when we are accepted and admired with doors of opportunity opening as a result. When the doors slam shut, we are aware of the rejection.

We are almost never aware of the doors that did not open because we were either disliked or simply not noticed. If our impression is negligible, if not invisible, people neither retreat from us nor embrace us. They just do not see us. We are forgotten without ever having a chance to be considered that sterling employee deserving promotion or that great lover deserving of an equally wonderful soul mate.

What is unforgettable about a good impression is the strength of character and the radiance of inner beauty. The strength reflects our discipline and success. The inner beauty mirrors our moral vehicle and how well we have taken care of the values that make up who we are. Even if we have been highly responsible for both our mental and moral vehicles, this brilliance can be held back by lack of self-knowledge, a diminished concept of who we are. A brilliant mental vehicle will be dulled by a poor moral one, as a successful professional can be ill mannered and socially vulgar.

To make a brilliant impression, the moral and mental vehicles must be working in unanimity. Then four conditions need to be met. We must:

- Be authentic and natural.
- Be receptive to people without judgements or expectations.
- Be respectful in manner and dress appropriately for the occasion.
- Give other people 100% of our attention.

AN AUTHENTIC IMPRESSION

IF WE THINK for a moment about individuals who have made beautiful and unforgettable impressions on us, we will remember that it was their whole demeanor that spoke to us—the way they handled themselves, their kindness to others, their topics of conversation, their choice of words, even the timbre of their voices. Everything they said or did stood out. But what probably struck us most was their obvious comfort in who they were. This is authenticity.

An authentic person can be described as being natural. The word natural may be misleading because it can mean common or easy, but being strong, truthful, unaffected and kind is rather extraordinary. Although a natural personality can be attained by anyone, it requires work and consistency.

A friend of mine named Alice is a business consultant who is often invited to speak to professional organizations. I was with her once when she was the guest speaker at a women's networking group. Sitting in the front row waiting for Alice to be introduced, we watched the proceedings of the group's regular meeting. The disrespect the president received was shocking. For a full half-hour the president loudly hushed her audience every few minutes, often hitting a glass with a spoon to demand attention, but the constant murmur continued. I whispered to Alice, "What are you going to do?" She calmly told me that if she received the same lack of consideration she would ask the 150 women present to raise their hands if they did not wish to listen to her. She would then invite them to leave and ask those who wanted to listen to remain. If no one wanted to stay, she would not impose herself any further, and she would withdraw with her dignity intact.

Finally amid the incessant noise, the president of the organization hastily introduced the guest speaker and with a look of utter relief stepped aside. Alice stood up, her posture balanced and poised, and walked to the microphone twenty feet from her seat with a stately stride. By the time she reached the podium, there was silence. Alice turned a pleasant countenance to her audience and began a forty-five minute presentation in which she held the entire room's attention.

After Alice's presentation, women crowded around her with questions and compliments. Curious why her reception was so different from the president's, I asked about a dozen women what it was in Alice's speech that they responded to. The dignity in her manner was the consensus. Some commented on how well Alice dressed. Others said that it would be rude not to pay attention to a guest, indicating the curious fact that we often give strangers better attention than those in whom we have more invested. Alice was described with words like "classy," "takes charge," "friendly," "magnetic" and "pleasant." All of them agreed that they had been impressed long before the lady opened her mouth.

I know the lady as a naturally calm individual, and she maintains her composure in crises because she has worked at being calm at all times. She is naturally respectful, having worked on giving consideration to herself and to others, those she liked and those she did not like. The dignity and poise with which she carries herself did not come naturally, but with the continuous effort of improving who she is. Her pleasant expression is a natural summation of her authenticity.

THE IMPORTANCE OF A PLEASANT EXPRESSION

AN EXPRESSION ENTAILS more than the features of our face. We express ourselves through body language, comments, ideas, and tone of voice, vocabulary, manners, care and so forth. The expression on our face will project the concept we have of ourselves. The responses elicited will match who we are. These would include respect, awe, excitement, interest, friendliness and acceptance on the positive side. And envy, resentment and rejection on the negative. People may react negatively to a person of high caliber if they have a low concept of themselves. Regardless, we must present our best at all times. Be authentic, be receptive, be well-mannered and be attentive. The considerate and respectful manner in which we treat others inspires similar pleasantry in return.

If we are thinking of our problems and perceive them as insurmountable, we project sadness, fear, anger or frustration. If we are working toward brilliance, problems are thought of as challenges, and we will reflect the determination to surpass them. Concentrating on what we are not or what we do not have is reflected by discontent and ingratitude. Happy or depressed, we make an impression according to our thoughts of the moment. While people may not be able to translate our facial expression into words, they will intuit a meaning and react with attraction, rejection or indifference.

THE SIGNIFICANCE OF EVERY ENCOUNTER

THE WELL KNOWN aphorism has it that the first impression is the most lasting, but that does not make it the most important. As we learned in our study of choices and responsibility, everything about who we are and what we do is significant. Our smallest act manifests our way of thinking. If we earn respect with our first impression, we must continue to earn it so that it does not fall into disrespect. In the quest for brilliance every impression we make is a first impression. In the stagnation of mediocrity we can close doors just as easily with a second or third or any number impression as we can with the first.

A bubbly and very attractive young woman named Erica came to see me for an initial consultation about taking classes.

She spoke with enthusiasm about herself and was for all appearances full of energy. Her energy was so hyper as to strike me as unnatural. I asked her what she wanted out of our work together. She said she didn't know. I asked her to tell me about her friends. She gave me a blank stare. I asked about her long-term relationships. She said she had none. That fit my impression of her. I would have been surprised if she kept friends longer that three months. Later in our conversation she admitted this was true.

For Erica, making great first impressions was easy, but to keep them was impossible. On the one hand she was always so happy to be with friends and was constantly doing things for them. On the other she was fiercely competitive and drained them with her constant demands for attention. When she relaxed, everyone became concerned that there was something wrong with her. Having no freedom to be herself, she was forced to move on to a new group of people, hoping for a new way of life, only to repeat the old pattern. She longed to break the cycle but had no alternate behavior.

Competing with others is not caused by insecurity alone but envy as well. Although Erica was beautiful, she envied the girls who were comfortable with themselves. I asked her about those feelings, and she was very direct in admitting them. "That is what I want to get rid of, the envy," she said. "I was afraid that you wouldn't see it, and I wouldn't have the courage to tell you. It's my big problem." I told her that I admired her for her honesty and that her problem was easy to fix. She burst into tears of relief and promised to do every bit of the homework I assigned.

I will get to solving the root cause of problems like Erica's in a moment. Years later at a social gathering a quiet and confident woman caught my eye, but I did not recognize Erica until she ran to greet me with a burst of effervescence. She was very happy and had made a wonderful group of friends whose companionship she increasingly nourished. As the result of her care, Erica received constant nourishment in return.

The gentle and natural manner Erica developed was more interesting than anything she could have pretended to be in the past. Then she wore a mask of a personality. It covered her insecurity for a short time, but eventually revealed that her attractiveness was phony. A false energy came out at once, all so shallow, a lot of noise and nothing to say. By just being who she was, she made people want to treat her well and take the time to know her better.

One of the things Erica learned is that life is a constant process of buying and selling. We buy with our self-worth. The impression that we make is the way we represent our worth. We make inadequate impressions by misrepresenting our value, either pretending to be more than we are or projecting less than we are. If we pretend and fail to sell the act, we are left depleted of energy, regretful and embarrassed. If we project less than we are, we suffer the feelings of diminishment and the loss of opportunities.

We rarely have a second opportunity to eradicate the unpleasant memory of a weak or offensive impression. A negative impression has a rippling effect on other opportunities. When people like what they see, they may tell ten others, but when they do not like what they see, they tell twenty more who repeat it to others until hundreds find out.

HOW TO BE FORGOTTEN

IF WE ARE not strong and positive, we will not connect with anyone. Making a weak impression is not offensive, but we will soon be forgotten.

Illustrative of this was Kelly, an extremely pretty young woman who came to see me because her boyfriend, one of my students, had ended their relationship abruptly. While I suggest that students postpone a decision about relationships until completing my three-month course, at which time they have more self-knowledge, some participants sever ties and neglect to tell me. In this case it was Kelly who informed me. She stated that she was very unhappy about it, but nothing in her manner suggested that she was particularly upset. She wanted to know what I had taught her boyfriend that had influenced him to break up with her. I emphasized that I do not give advice or tell people what to do. I just teach them how to think clearly. Then I offered Kelly a free hour to give her tools to improve some of her weak areas.

"You can't help me," she said in a flat voice, "because I already do all of the things you teach. I work for a highly successful law firm, have a position of responsibility, and I am doing very well. Not to brag about it, but I wear fashionable clothes, drive a sports car, live at a good address, and I am thankful for all of it."

Through hard work and dedication Kelly obviously had accumulated many accomplishments, for which I respected her. As she continued, it was clear that she also recognized and respected her mental vehicle. Yet with all her monetary success, diplomas and physical beauty, she was very bland. When I asked her what kind of impression she made on people in general, she answered in a matter-of-fact tone: "None. I am the person everyone forgets as soon as I leave the room."

Honesty is always disarming. Kelly was typical of high caliber people who are aware of what they are worth intellectually but have no sense of their personal values and project themselves as much less in quality than they are. Without growing in our being, we are going to reach a place of stagnation no matter how much we know or how efficient we are at what we do.

"I can help you," I told her. "You have taken your mental vehicle, your work and service, to a point of excellence. But you have not done the same with your being, your moral vehicle, the essence of who you are. If you do not raise the quality of your choices in the personal aspect, it will stunt your career. You do not make an impression because you project no energy, no vibrancy. Your personality is dull. Not because you are dull but because you do not project dignity. Instead, you probably compromise to please others. No one respects that, and you are alienating the very people you want to cultivate."

Kelly responded, "I identify with what you are saying. I've had many thoughts about it, but I couldn't put them into words. Will you work with me?"

We worked well together. Kelly had taken her values for granted because she could not identify them. Once she learned the information in the last chapter, she began to use her values responsibly. Instead of being taken advantage of, she began to receive the respect she gave and the consideration she deserved in return. Aware of her values and especially how she used them, she could easily identify the moment when someone would try to impose on her. In a refined manner she began to let people know when their actions were not acceptable. Most would apologize and take a step back; others would accuse her of being too sensitive. Soon a free, bright and warm personality began to emerge. New perspectives and attitudes replaced old concepts. The value Kelly placed on her professional services increased as it became congruent with the value she placed on her personal worth. With her moral and mental vehicles humming along side by side, she gave quality to every aspect of her life. I had no doubt that she would advance to new opportunities.

Several years later at a restaurant I saw a vaguely familiar woman who turned out to be Kelly. The beautiful but forgettable girl of our first encounter had blossomed into a stunning lady. Her life had taken on new dimensions with exciting opportunities opening around her. She was off to Texas to grow in a new job that made the old one look dismal by comparison. As for her old boyfriend, she had no regrets that he had rejected her.

FOR EVERY CHOICE THERE IS A REJECTION

KELLY USED REJECTION to change her life. One of the impressive characteristics of strong and positive people is how they deal with apparent negatives. Every time we make a choice, we reject one thing in favor of another thing. Viewed with clarity, rejection should be a non-threatening experience. We cannot expect to be liked by everyone anymore than we can expect to be prepared to take all the opportunities available. When we were in elementary school learning long division, we had no problem that we were not selected to take algebra exams. Why is it that later in life we often feel badly when we are not selected for opportunities we are not yet fully prepared for? Although there is pain when people we wish to accept us reject us, the benefits can far outweigh the bruising of our ego.

If our conduct has caused rejection, then we have the opportunity to surpass something in ourselves, use the experience for learning, make a determination to correct it permanently and move on.

Remember that it is possible to be rejected for exhibiting elevated behavior. It is common to be disliked by the envious, and it is foolish to continue in their company. Rejection is undignified if it is done with disrespect, but mostly the indignity is choosing to stay where we know we are not appreciated.

As for being tolerated, I should rather choose rejection every time. To be constantly tolerated is to live in humiliation. We are acknowledged only to the point of not being ignored but count for nothing without ever being rejected. There is no dignity if we remain where we know we are tolerated. There is dignity only if we withdraw.

The fear of making a bad impression is ever present for many of us but not as difficult to conquer as it appears. A worse fear is making such a weak impression that we might as well be invisible.

Making a weak impression is due to the weak or poor exposure of our values. When we are fearful, we anxiously wonder, What are other people going to think about me? Regrettably, most people do not think of anyone else except themselves. Being worried about ourselves is the equivalent of being so conceited that we do not care about others. Whether we are shy or arrogant, we disconnect from people if we do not think about them, and when we disconnect, they do not see us.

If we think we are uninteresting, we will look boring. Why then would anyone want to meet us?

HOW TO BE INTERESTING

ONE OF MY students Sarah told me that her best friend Ruth had become resentful of her. Their most recent conflict had to do with the impression Sarah made on others. Ruth said, "I hate what you do. You always act like you are the favorite wherever we go." I asked Sarah what she thought about when she met people.

"Oh nothing," she said. "I never think about anything right when I'm meeting someone. I just give them my full attention and try to make them feel at ease the best way that I can. I enjoy people. I'm very lucky," she added. "People like me."

It is clear to us now that taking care of people is a strong choice of conviction, and when coupled with 100% attention or effort, great success is assured. In Sarah's case success translated into favorable impressions. The consequences of her choices and efforts had nothing to do with her being very lucky, but with responsibility. When applied to our treatment of people, the Law of Responsibility tells us that the impressions we make are not accidental but due to the attention we put into them. By treating others as favorites of our immediate attention, they respond with pleasure and appreciation.

Another example of how this works was my music teacher. She had many qualities that made her very much loved by her students. The one that stood out for me was that she made me feel like I was her favorite student. She gave me her full attention and seemed to enjoy every minute of her time with me. Her admonishments sounded like encouragement, and even when she was disciplining me, I felt that she cared deeply for my well being. When she died suddenly, I was shocked and grieved. At the memorial service at least seventy-five of her students made the unique claim of being her special friend and most favorite student. I refrained from setting them straight, not wanting to cause jealousy, and my discretion saved me from utterly embarrassing myself!

By a blessed turn of events, I met my teacher's daughter years later. Like her mother, the daughter became my great supporter. She has been personally responsible for the expansion of my work. She introduced me to her many friends. Each one is convinced that she is the daughter's very best friend.

When we apply responsibility to all areas of our life, appreciation becomes a gift that is naturally bestowed. It becomes an attitude, a way of being that we project. From moment to moment we project our thoughts, and if we are projecting the choice and effort to care for people, they immediately sense it and react to it.

THE BURDEN OF PRETENSION

IT IS ONE thing to impress by being authentic and projecting the natural majesty of an elevated soul. It is quite another to try to impress with the arrogance that says, "You are not as important as I am." This should be interpreted as a form of rejection, but if we submit to the imposition in any way, we are giving tacit agreement that the person's grand view of himself is true. We may even flatter ourselves with the notion that he must think we are important enough to impress because he would not bother if we were insignificant. If we accept this image as true, we feed his false sense of power, the sole purpose of which is to diminish us. It is the only way he can stand out.

To distinguish between the authentic and the false, it helps to remember that a person who is authentic never needs to show off. He avoids it completely. Showing off and exaggerating are for those who are living in mediocrity. To accept a performance as real makes us vulnerable because we are reacting to and believing the theatrics, not the reality of the person behind the act. We create expectations that the owner of the image cannot keep.

For people functioning in mediocrity or below, it is safe to say that half are busy trying to impress and that the other half are being impressed. Either way their behavior gives away the level of thought they live in. When you are in the presence of human beings that live with brilliance, you know it immediately because the tranquillity and gentleness of their authenticity puts you at ease. We are accepted and not judged. Because we all share the imperfections of being human, there is no absolute way to determine the level of growth where each of us is. To achieve authenticity and avoid being deceived, it is prudent neither to believe nor disbelieve what we see. Simply watch. We must always be respectful, allow people to be who they are and not be unkind to them. It is harder for them to live with who they are than it is for us to meet them with our best.

No one creates a false image unless he dislikes or hates himself. These negative feelings come from fear of rejection and shame at lack of accomplishment. In the worst cases pretenders end up manifesting envy, greed, covetousness, compulsive lying and a need to steal or destroy.

The pain of feeling inadequate is what first compels people to hide behind images. They create the image of what they would like to be, or at least what they think it should look like, and this costume becomes the most important aspect of them. It is their whole impression. So critical is this false image that it is usually taken to a perverse perfection. They are obsessively loyal to the image and demand to be treated as they believe the image should be. Then they feel betrayed and disrespected when they are not. Ironically, were they loyal to the values that the false image represents, they would be better off because with time they would grow into the image and surpass it with authentic gifts.

No matter how good the image gets, it is still an act. An act is always self-limiting. The person pretending to be what he is not cannot take advantage of an opportunity when it is presented because, if he cannot maintain the act, he will be discovered. The act will never fool those who are at higher levels intellectually or morally. How long can the pretender put on his show without showing results? The act grows old. It is what we have done or not done that begins to speak for us. We can only talk so long of what we are going to do. One day we have to show something if we are to be believed.

People enveloped in their act suffer the fear of being discovered. When they are inevitably exposed, they suffer guilt and humiliation. If they continue to live without responsibility, they will give in to the need to compensate and end up envying those who live with more effort. Rather than resent such misguided and wasted individuals, we should feel compassion for them. They want so much to be admired, but those they try to impress grow to pity or only tolerate them. Pity is not born out of respect but of contempt. An image works only when there is still time left for wishful thinking. The eventual awakening always brings despair.

At the end of their lives false personalities have nothing to show for their productive years. Their bitterness at what life dealt them makes them unbearable as company, and it is too late for them to begin something worthwhile because they have not built the strength of character to sustain any positive effort. People do start and succeed at new ventures very late in life but usually because they have exercised a high degree of responsibility throughout their lives.

THE DANGERS OF FALSE IMAGES

I HAVE WORKED with some people, not many, who could have stepped out of their false personalities before it was too late but chose to continue the farce. They would burst into tears at the thought of letting go of their image because they would feel naked without it. After all, it takes a lot of time and work to make a convincing costume. But it is our soul (the essence of our moral vehicle) and our service (the work encompassed by our mental vehicle) that God has given us to reveal brilliantly. To perfect a man made image is a fool's waste of effort feeding pride.

Pride is the root cause of many evils. Rebellion from all that is good follows, and envy and greed grow stronger and stronger. Greed and envy are terminal diseases. People sometimes get better but usually do not heal completely although, as with other terminal diseases, a few do. In my experience these few cure themselves both with great effort and by turning to God in deep prayer. They go through wrenching changes that convert their values from the material to the spiritual.

The ones who improve somewhat learn to rein in their negative qualities at least some of the time while yielding to them the rest. They may go to church regularly and delude themselves into thinking that they are spiritual, but what they are after or have acquired is mostly what other people have created. The accumulation of material goods can never bring them the peace and happiness they desire, nor can they fully enjoy what they have, if at all. The following are three object lessons about remaining unhealed.

Brigitte had a pretty face and at first impression a pleasant personality. I soon learned that she had copied what she found charming in other women and accumulated all their "cute" expressions into what she regarded as a unique, self-centered reality. To make matters a bit more complicated for her, her best friend had accumulated the same cute traits. When I had them both in front of me as prospective students, I mentioned their similarities and asked who was copying whom.

"Oh," Brigitte said, "we are very competitive, and we love it because it keeps our friendship alive."

I never heard such nonsense, but both girls signed up with me anyway. The friend healed herself by working on continuous self-correction to accomplish her moral and mental goals. Later she met and married an ambitious young man, and together they created a lovely family. Brigitte meanwhile kept looking for a man to marry, but she did not attract what she wanted. At the age of forty she made up her mind to become more aggressive. She was going to catch a wealthy man whether he was single or not. Sure enough, she enticed a rich man away from his wife and moved in with him while he made up his mind whether to remarry. Part of the reason for his delay was Brigitte's thinking it was unfair for the estranged wife to keep so much of the community property. Due to Brigitte's suggestions, the divorce proceedings lasted much longer than they needed.

After a messy settlement a triumphant Brigitte was now ready to get married. But she had a new problem. Seeing what she was capable of conniving for the sake of keeping money, her lover decided he would get married only if she signed a prenuptial agreement that would strictly limit her claims to his wealth. Brigitte refused. The last I heard, she was considering suing him because he had taken so much of her time.

The second unhealed case was that of a man who perfected the act of playing Don Juan. He garnished his performance with charming little sayings that he collected from the naive women who are attracted to sexual predators. He bragged that he was irresistible to women and had conquered more than three hundred. Some supported him financially, but he didn't stay attached for longer than six months. Investing so much of himself into being a seducer, he had little left over for any meaningful relationship or job. At fifty he has no friends and no career, and is well on his way to becoming a desiccated and shriveled caricature of what he used to be.

Finally there was a man named Robert who introduced himself as Bobby. I immediately commented that a nickname, especially such a diminutive one, did not inspire much confidence in his abilities as the CEO of an international company. A nickname is appropriate for a ten-year-old boy but not for a man of Robert's stature. I asked him to tell me about his accomplishments. He replied that he had graduated from university with highest honors. "And how did you celebrate?" I asked.

"I didn't," he said. When I asked him why, his answer explained his unhappiness. "Because I stole the tests." As we continued, he revealed that all his accomplishments had been attained dishonestly, from cheating for grades in class to the latest acquisition made by his company. We cannot live forever with appearances; within ourselves we live with what we know we are; and at this point in his life Robert said he wanted to change. He made tremendous improvements, but he could not eradicate his envy and his greed. When I told him he had to try his best to let go of his image and be authentic, tears flowed from his eyes as he cried out, "Then I'm nothing."

It is never pleasant to watch people look at themselves and find that they do not like what they see. Robert was honest with me and with himself in acknowledging that he did not have the courage to give up the lies he had been living his whole life. He wanted to set aside manipulation and cheating the next time he embarked on a new project. Wanting something, however, is far different from determining to do it.

Predictably, Robert chose to stay in his act, and it caught up with him. His company is much smaller now and barely surviving. The prognosis is never good when you are mired in mediocrity.

THE UNFORGETTABLE IMPRESSION

SINCE THE LARGEST group of people live in the mediocre or inferior levels of thought, the vast majority of the impressions we are exposed to are negative. Most people come across as weak, dull or offensive.

Like anyone else, those who live in lower levels also have a need to stand out, but since they cannot do it on their own, they do it at others' expense and are adept at unfair competition. Outer manifestations are vulgarity and disrespect. The worst of the impressions we wish we could forget but cannot are the destructive ones. They come in the form of unkindness, cruelty and covert or overt violence. Rarely are rough people confronted with their cruelty. They are feared and tolerated for a while until they can be avoided altogether.

There are many good people who live in mediocrity who are not motivated by the desires to deceive and degrade, but their basic insecurity nevertheless compels them to hide who they are and be phony. Many make fools of themselves just for the sake of being remembered, and they are but not with pleasure. One chooses to proclaim his imagined virtues while another plays the clown. Some try to make their mark through pedantry; others hope to impress by bragging about material possessions, experiences or social connections. To make a memorable impression, they pay the price of being ridiculous.

Others are shy and weak but good people who make no impression at all. At least they cause no damage and do not pretend to be more than what they are.

As we saw with Kelly, the same duality exists among higher caliber people when they take their values for granted. They think their good qualities are natural, therefore normal, and waste no time attributing them to others. We have mentioned before that by assuming values in others we automatically set ourselves up for disappointment and betrayal. We base our expectations on what we imagine to be true. This is why many people fall in love with a false image, or with the projection of their own values. Then they spend a tremendous amount of time arguing or demanding that the pretender fall back on the fraudulent behavior of the initial impression. People believe that men or women change after marriage. I believe that they change at courtship, and after marriage they revert to who they really are.

Impressions are moment by moment events. Imagine seeing a woman driving erratically and at high speed at two o'clock in the morning. She is running red lights, forcing other cars up on the sidewalk. Some people honk their horns and shout obscenities at her. You might think that the woman is crazy because that is the impression she gives. She continues to break the speed limit for miles and miles. All the way to the hospital.

She brings the car to a screeching halt, parks and pushes open her door. She rushes to the passenger side and scoops a baby out of his safety seat. He is rasping for breath, his lips blue and his eyes pleading. The terrified woman carries him in her arms and runs to the entrance of the emergency room, thinking that each agonized breath will be the boy's last.

Inside, a dedicated pediatrician is waiting. His eyes look puffy from being awakened from a sound sleep. He too has broken a few traffic laws to get to the hospital quickly.

Scenes like the above were repeated with nightmarish frequency during my younger son's first eight years of life. Mercifully, he grew out of the condition that would have me from time to time giving the impression of a mad woman or a delinquent running away from the police.

Any impression offers the temptation of immediate judgment, but things are not always as they appear. We must force ourselves to take the time to arrive at an informed opinion. If we refrain from the judgment of the moment, we will be protected from ignorance, getting hurt and being manipulated.

Holding off from judgment is not thoughtless or passive. We are to watch what unfolds. As we watch, we begin to see what repeats is consistent and can be believed. When attitudes repeat in different manifestations and situations, they reveal the truth of the person behind them. The aspects that are authentic will continue to improve and shine. The more you know an authentic person the more you will like him. The more you know a superficial or false person the less you will like him.

By accepting appearances as truth, we establish ourselves as naive and judgmental. Naiveté places us in danger; being judgmental makes us dangerous. The blind trust of naiveté is not attractive unless it is in the delightful innocence of a very young person. As we mature, awareness, sharpness of mind and wit are what we want to cultivate. To be judgmental is a form of character assassination. Unless checked, this attitude becomes a habit, and we will become known as critical and opinionated.

WE ARE ALL THAT WE DO

WE ARE OUR posture, energy, gestures, and choice of personal possessions and how we take care of them. We are our thoughts and voice and vocabulary and topics of conversation. We are our responses and reactions to situations, people, opinions and things. Every nuance of us constitutes the palette of our personality from which the complete portrait of us is painted. People can wear designer clothes or clever make up, but these can never cover the real picture. We are not attractive when we speak badly of someone. If we harbor negativity, we cannot have a pleasant expression. Clothing and workouts notwithstanding, how we think and feel will manifest physically. Positive and negative.

I remember reading about how Leonardo daVinci created *The Last Supper.* Artists do not invent faces. An imagined face, though anatomically correct, would be devoid of soul, so daVinci searched diligently for real life models whose faces embodied the overriding quality that was the very essence of each apostle. The last and most difficult model to find was the one for Judas. His face was pivotal to the painting, and it needed to be remarkable for the treachery it tried to mask.

Finally da Vinci found the perfect face. The man greeted him as if they had already met. The master did not recognize him at first, but this man had posed for him many years before for the same painting. He had stood for St. John, the joyous young apostle whom Jesus called beloved.

PROJECTING A BETTER IMAGE

YOUR FIRST STEPS to making a beautiful and lasting impression have already been taken as you completed the exercises in the previous chapters. You learned that most people think and live in mediocrity or below, and by that alone they are the least equipped to pass judgment. Their opinions have little or no value. With these realizations you are no longer vulnerable to most impressions. You no longer have to take the opinions and

pretensions of others as a personal affront, and you are less vulnerable to flattery or belittlement.

This frees you to use your new knowledge of what an
impression is. You know that the only impression with value is
an authentic one, one that is strong but gentle. You realize that
you are always making a first impression even when you are
meeting people you already know.

Respect for others is your responsibility, but do not compare yourself to them nor consider that their interests are more
important than your own for they are not.

Acceptance of our present growth gives us a stronger presence and allows us to be more genuine. As you complete your
Five Acts of Improvement each day and take more responsibility
for your moral and mental vehicles, the impression you make cannot help but improve, and eventually it will shine brilliantly.

Following are five ways to further polish your impression.
Include them as you wish as part of your Five Acts of
Improvement.

1. Eliminate from your body language any action that you
    identify as unnatural, including affectations of gesture and
    speech you may have incorporated over the years.

2. Improve your facial expression. The most important aspect
    of an attractive body language is a pleasant facial expression.
    If you have difficulty presenting a pleasant facial expression,
    the following exercise will help you.

    •   Stand in front of the mirror, or use your video camera
        to record yourself, and bring to mind a circumstance in
        your life that causes you pain. Note your expression.
        This is the expression that you wear when you have
        unhappy thoughts.

- Bring to mind someone or something that causes you happiness and note your expression. Turn away from the mirror or camera and become familiar with the way this expression of happiness feels.
- Face the mirror again to see if you still have the expression of happiness. This is the expression you are to wear.

3. Tone down loud noises, from unseemly laughter to banging things around, and moderate your voice and gestures so that they are not abrupt or abrasive.

4. Do not lean on furniture except when you are sitting, and do not lean on walls. Never slouch.

5. Meet people with the thought of taking pleasure in their company. Give all of your attention to the person with whom you are speaking. Keep good eye contact and open up your heart.

Some of these exercises may not feel natural at first because they are a new way of conducting yourself. These are the manifestations of a new way of thinking that you are still learning. Already you convey your natural personality at will when you express feelings of compassion at a funeral or feelings of joy at a wedding or other celebrations.

Being authentic never means that we can impose on others whatever we feel, and that includes our problems, our negative reactions or our bad manners. Imposing our every attitude on others is a sure way to make a lasting impression, one that you undoubtedly do not wish to make.

When Dreams
Come True

"SOMETHING THAT IS exactly as one desires" is one
dictionary's very attractive definition of an ideal. Related defini-
tions point to the dual nature of an ideal, how it is both a concept of mind and that which externally fulfills the concept. An
ideal starts as the highest possible perception that we can imagine for someone or something. When the perceived ideal is
embodied in an object, a situation, a person or a behavior, the
realized ideal is the zenith of workmanship, the best that one
can be, an expression of truth and beauty.

We can claim as many of these beautiful expressions as we
desire through the constant effort of driving our moral and
mental vehicles toward perfection, simultaneously, each with
equal strength. We saw in Chapter 4 that learning how to do
something well, even with high quality, is not enough.

We may have been born with a good soul and obvious talents, but we have a moral obligation of refining and elevating our virtues and gifts every day, and adding to them whenever we can. We never know what brilliance lies one baby step from our present ability. We do know that God's ideal was called into being as a perfect universe in which there is an intelligent design and beautiful purpose for every human being. He created us with the abilities to accomplish our ideals, blessing us with the moral and mental gifts of a mind and body to manifest them. He included free will so that at any moment we can choose to fit into the brilliance intended for us, turn away from it or sit down and do nothing. What we contribute to God's high purpose and the style of how we do it are different for each of us, but the ideals of contributing and getting better at it are the same for everyone.

Ideals are conceived and brought to fruition daily through our Five Acts of Improvement. In them we define and polish our work, service and quality of being. Through this improvement we awaken other talents, skills and strengths, not the least of which is the energy and desire to accomplish more. Some invigorating qualities and talents may lie so deep as to be dormant at the moment, but they are intimately part of us, waiting to be discovered. As we reach new plateaus of growth, new opportunities and challenges allow us to call forth new strengths from our ever-expanding potential.

Wealth and fame are sometimes measurements of a job well done, but they are merely variables in the potential promised by the full utilization of our moral and mental vehicles. Fame can be an agreeable experience, but it is nothing compared to self-respect. With or without wealth we all must contribute in some way. The fundamental constants consist of imbuing the contributions of our work and our service, ourselves and our relationships with responsibility and gratitude. These are what will make us happy.

The worth of our contributions depends on how finely we conceptualize ideals and how expertly we realize them. We always have more than one set of circumstances to bring to bear our ideals, and for most of us these include:

- Work, chores or study, occupation or profession
- Relationships, familial and otherwise
- Special gifts and talents, interests and projects
- Virtues and qualities of character

Even in a minimal job at the lowest pay, we can contribute the ideals of doing our best, inspiring those around us and not complaining about the management. When we give our best in present circumstances, we surpass the level we are in, exercise imagination and initiative, and accumulate other strengths, all of which are necessary to fulfilling any ideal.

Steven, a nineteen-year-old freshman at university, had been depressed for six months over choosing a major. His first love was anthropology, but he had studied reports on the most financially promising careers, and anthropology was not anywhere near the top. The ones that were had no appeal to him, and he felt doomed. If he followed his heart, he feared he would not earn enough money.

I suggested that he sign up for his favorite, anthropology. "But do not expect it or any other subject to open doors of opportunity. It is the quality of effort that you put into your education that unlocks your potential. You could discover applications of anthropology to marketing, communications, international development, fields in which you could become a highly paid consultant and could end up a popular lecturer or a best-selling author. You might discover a love for academic research that surpasses any desire you have now for a specific amount of money. You may even decide to change majors, but right now your job is to make a choice and build your character on it. What you know is not nearly as important as the strengths you acquire pursuing the knowledge."

Steven needed to know that the opportunities for growth do not begin when we decide what we want to do with our lives. We discover what we want to do as the result of growth. This is the Law of Responsibility at work. If you are putting it into practice and have not yet found your calling in life, that means your potential is higher than your strengths at the moment, not that you lack gifts or talents. A dormant or weak interest may be an undiscovered gift that requires serious effort to develop into a talent.

The alternative to doing our best today is to remain in distress or anger, to stagnate and wait for something to happen rather than making it happen. We know that stagnation takes us only to the next level of complaint.

OUR IDEALS, OUR PURPOSE

WEAK CHARACTER PREVENTS most people from reaching their ideals. Lack of grace prevents some of those who achieve their ideals in the mental area from sharing and enjoying them.

Most people choose to develop only their mental vehicle. Ideals center around their profession, which they may spiritualize by describing it as a mission or a calling, but it cannot have spiritual value unless it is simultaneously developed with the moral vehicle. Achieving excellence only in a career creates imbalance. A career can isolate a person's identity to the point that it does not exist outside of his profession. Often when that person comes home, he does not have any human values to offer as a spouse or a parent. The moral vehicle, weak from lack of use, is on its way to atrophy.

Careers, occupations and hobbies are important, and are responsible for half of our success and happiness. But they are only half of our potential.

This imbalance is a defect of character, not because of what is missing, but because of what is ignored. We can try and over-compensate with even more success, but it will not supplant the moral need. To favor one over the other is to be always off balance and to limp continually in mediocrity. How does a person with only a strong mental drive manage challenges that require great moral strength? Or vice versa?

This imbalance shows in prayer. Often we pray for the things that we want, not for what we need. Instead of praying for growth in all aspects, which would bring all kinds of benefits, we pray for material things and then suffer when we do not get them. Praying for growth will never lead to disappointment because we always gain strength as we grow.

THE IMPORTANCE OF IDEALS

TEENAGERS AND YOUNG adults often complain that they do not know what they want to do with their lives. The lack of vision is often the result of not working with either vehicle.

At an early age we learn to use our mental vehicle by picking up after ourselves and studying, and our moral vehicle by the way we treat our relationships. As the years go by we learn more about what we do, with final exams and graduations serving as milestones. We develop who we are with guidance from our family and friends. Growth comes quickly when we are young because every year marks a new level of knowledge and experience. The next level is always in sight. I have concluded that something happens when we leave school and the family home to begin our independent lives. The planning stops. The work stops. Suddenly we believe our lives are without purpose.

Youth's accumulated experiences prepare us to move up with optimism. Wisdom and desire intertwine to create a rope that we climb up and up to a place where potential and ideals are always expanding. The more strengths and values we accumulate, the greater our access to brilliance.

Many of my students come to me and reveal that their life has no direction. Ideals are the framework upon which we define purpose and plan how to achieve it. Without ideals our plans will fall onto the floor in a heap. At minimum we have a comfortable place to sit and dream.

DREAMS VS. IDEALS

BETWEEN AN IDEAL and a dream yawns a chasm. Many people fall into it because they confuse the two sides. They have healthy desires for a better life and good intentions about achieving them. The problem is that they do not take action to turn desire and intention into reality. Not because they do not want to, but because they are overwhelmed and do not know how to begin.

An ideal is a God-given idea that we take responsibility for and make our best effort to accomplish. A dream, on the other hand, is a wish that we carry unfulfilled until its dead weight crushes our spirit. Ideals are brilliant and active; dreams are pretty pictures and nothing more.

The readers of this book who are doing their Five Acts of Improvement are idealists, moving toward an elevated outcome whether they recognize it or not. The Five Acts renew energy, create clarity and plant seeds of thought that are germinating into a whole new way of seeing life's potential.

Life is energy that demands to be spent. It can be spent talking about dreams. It can be spent fantasizing about them. It can be spent fretting about what needs to be done and frightening oneself about where to start. Daydreaming is healthy for creating ideas, but to fantasize is a waste of time. Over time those pretty dreams get crowded out with doubts. The soul's instinct for brilliance turns the dreamer's unfulfilled potential into a severe inquisitor. Have I ever claimed what is available for me? Am I a failure? A coward? The dreamer sees brilliance in others around him, and it makes him envious, not so much for what they have, but for the ability to create it. Were he desirous of the labor behind success, he would be able to manifest his own abundance.

Envy, greed and coveting feed the dreamer's anger. The denial of all responsibility allows for other escapes, resenting others and plotting reprisals. The anger is really toward himself. There is shame for choosing to survive doing the minimum rather than for flourishing at doing the maximum. As with any victim, the dreamer's life becomes a total of "some"s. Someday my ship will come. Someone will discover me and make me rich and famous. Some magical event will happen and make my life like Cinderella's.

What is forgotten about the fairy tale is that Cinderella lived with the choices of an idealist long before she knew there was a prince or had any hope of getting out of her slavery. Under the yoke of two envious stepsisters, she did not condemn them. Instead she kept busy doing what needed to be done to the best of her ability. In the process she developed her royal qualities. Cinderella was an aristocratic soul without a title. The carriage, the jewels and the glass slippers only made her look like a princess. Her majesty was in the depth of her being. This is what the prince fell in love with, searched for and rediscovered when she had no outer finery. Had Cinderella's sisters followed her commitment to brilliance, their own beautiful personalities would have unfolded, and they would have attracted their own hearts' desires. Instead they did nothing except fantasize and envy.

HOW DREAMS BECOME IDEALS

INADVERTENTLY WE SOMETIMES play roles in the encouragement of others' dreams even if at the moment our contribution may appear as negative and unpleasant.

I had just arrived in the United States after a speaking tour in Latin America. I was jet lagged, physically tired but restless of mind, and accepted an invitation to a Christmas party that evening, seduced by the thought of listening to others and not having to speak. Because of the looming New Year, conversations were full of resolutions and plans. I met a lady who said she was going to open a boutique. I became interested and posed the natural questions. What kind of boutique? Where? What type of items was she going to sell? Large or small objects? Local handcrafts or imported?

She had no idea.

How long had she had this dream?

"Ten years."

What had she done for her boutique so far?

"Nothing."

Any research?

"No, but I am going to."

She knew what I did for a living and requested my opinion.

I asked her if she wanted a social opinion or my professional opinion. Professional, she said. I gave it. She would never open a boutique based on the fact that she had done nothing about it. She was furious and told me that I was mistaken. Confrontation with one's truth is sometimes painful, a thought that I kept to myself, as well as the thought that we both had made a mistake—she for inviting my opinion and I for giving it.

Several years later I was standing in the checkout line at my supermarket when someone called my name. I turned to face a lady smiling broadly at me. While I am not famous, I speak to many groups, and I do not have the gift of remembering all of the faces, much less the names. I asked her to please help me place her.

"I was that woman at that Christmas party. I never forgot you. You were right, saying what I already knew, that I would never open my boutique since I had done nothing about it. I hated what you said because it brought out all of my fears. For three days I could not stop thinking about your words and how I needed to do something however small."

Then from her purse she took out a beautifully engraved invitation announcing the opening of her boutique. The radiance in her face spoke for the accomplishment of her ideal.

Most people already have plans and are following them in some manner, but they have not drawn a formal course of action. Some have desires but are not doing anything about them. Others have no idea of what they want to do with their lives and are not making any choices. A few have defined their plans by charting what to do, and then they take action until completion. The last group will reach their highest potential.

I believe that we need to start with a chart of our ideals if we are to go beyond our dreams. In making a chart we begin to see the milestones we must meet and the pitfalls we must avoid. For any navigator a chart is indispensable for a safe and successful journey.

HOW TO DEFINE YOUR IDEALS

CHOOSE YOUR MOST daring dream to turn into an ideal and do not be concerned with the question, What if that is not what I really want to do? You can always change destinations at any time, but you will take your experience, insights, strength and courage with you and succeed in what you finally want to do. In achieving the utmost for ourselves, the journey should be pleasant with medium goals and small goals. They should be recognizable and accessible.

Instead of starting at the first step, we are going straight to the last step, our outcome, the dream, as if it is already an accomplished fact. From there we are going to map our steps backward and review the challenges and goals as if we had already met them. Now the chart will be like reliving the experience. With the confident advantage of hindsight, we can set aside any fears about what we will encounter on the way.

Pause and consider your mental vehicle for the moment. What is the highest possible level you could take your service to, and choose that as an ideal. For the purpose of clarity we will do a chart for one ideal at a time as you may have more than one dream in this area.

Having chosen the acme of your desires, you can begin to recognize the completed goals before your success. Start with any number—my favorite is five—and ask yourself, "Can I do any of them today?" If you can, they are tasks. If you cannot, they are goals. Now choose one of the goals and repeat the process to recognize the last five steps that made it happen. If you can do any of these steps today, you have found your task or tasks of the day; if not, you are facing another set of goals. It is not necessary that all the goals possible appear on your chart. Start with the ones you recognize now; others will reveal themselves when you are already moving on your journey.

TASKS OF THE DAY

THE KEY TO opening your potential is the task of the day. Each goal is built upon successively smaller goals until the smallest task is revealed. It makes no difference how many dreams you want to take to ideals. The task of the day is always easy to do now.

The choices that we make to create an ideal are simple, small and subtle acts. Taken in natural progression, they forge a strong chain of acts that complete a goal. The accumulation of these goals embraces the entire ideal. People get stranded trying to figure out the radical step that is going to take them to their ideal. They cannot see the immediate step because they are thinking about the outcome. And it is the outcome, not the step, that is radical.

Each small goal represents a comfortable landmark on the journey. Comfortable is the key word here. An individual may have the ideal to lose fifty pounds. Five pounds a week is not a comfortable goal and therefore not sustainable. It is more comfortable and beneficial to lose one pound per week and sustain it than to lose fifteen pounds in three weeks and gain them all back. The purpose is not only to lose the weight but also to build the habits that will maintain a healthier life. A marathon runner does not begin by running 26 miles a day but slowly builds from five miles to ten miles and so on. To a thirteen-year-old student whose ideal is a Ph. D. in engineering, his landmark may be to complete his freshman year of high school, with the immediate goal of preparing for a history exam, while his tasks of the day are keeping up with his homework. To avoid giving up from moral, mental or physical fatigue, the steps must be comfortable and taken at your own pace, but they must be continuous.

The chart below is a generalized example of starting with an ideal and working backward to a single task.

Goals/Tasks

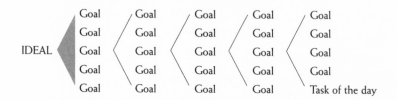

IDEAL	Goal	Goal	Goal	Goal	Goal
	Goal	Goal	Goal	Goal	Goal
	Goal	Goal	Goal	Goal	Goal
	Goal	Goal	Goal	Goal	Goal
	Goal	Goal	Goal	Goal	Task of the day

You will do more and get to your desired destination faster with a chart than without it. What is more, with your chart you not only surpass yourself but also discover even higher ideals. Keep your chart where you can see it. Some of the goals will be long term; others, more immediately achievable. By seeing them all at once you can recognize any opportunity to do a task for any goal, sometimes for one that might have seemed far off.

My original ideal was not defined in writing a book. It was to fulfill a moral obligation to bring this education to the public. As a speaker and teacher I thought that I could train teachers. After trying that for several years and failing miserably, I decided that I would write all the information down as a correspondence course, but then my ideal changed to writing this book.

To illustrate the application of clearly defining ideals and charting a plan of action, allow me to share the process of completing the book you are holding.

Publish Book Chart

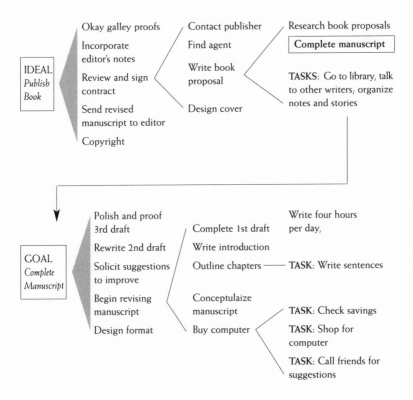

I did another chart to map how to earn a living while I wrote. I contracted some people to organize groups to whom I could speak and others who could get me media coverage. With the chart I could see where I could set aside time for writing. That time translated into the sentences and pages that were the daily ongoing tasks of the ideal of publishing.

The goal of producing a proposal was completed before the manuscript. As I got closer to finishing the manuscript, I began contacting publishers. All of the famous houses turned me down.

I was in this process when I mentioned it to a student, a vice president of an entertainment company. His ideal was to publish non-fiction books that would enrich people's lives, and he had been looking for a product for about a year. We began our work together almost immediately.

A suggestion here to insure peace of mind on your journey. Keep your ideals and your plan of action private, divulging only as much as you need to gather information, because once you have spoken, you are vulnerable to discussion. Ideals are intimate. You do not need people mocking your lofty aspirations.

THE OPPORTUNITY OF THE MOMENT

IN THE ABSENCE of well-defined ideals, it is easy to create a chart of your present work and idealize the opportunity of the moment. It is not important that you do not like what you do because I will show you how to use it as transportation to brilliance. If you do not have a job or occupation, begin to look for something whether it brings income or not. By idealizing your present situation, you will develop new skills, new qualities and strengths. At the same time you will be developing a new way of thinking that will carry you to your next level of growth and the new opportunities you are likely to encounter.

Some years ago my student Marie brought her sister Kathleen to see me for a few sessions. Kathleen had just had an unfortunate turn of events and had moved from the Midwest to California with her four daughters to begin a new life. She was on welfare, and she wanted out of it. Because Marie wanted to help her, I suggested that Marie put up a Work Wanted sign at a church mission she supported. The mission needed a secretary and hired Kathleen immediately. I suggested that she elevate her work to brilliance by doing much more than was required and wait to see what would happen. Within a few months the sisters at the mission could not stop talking about Kathleen and about how grateful they were for her good-natured efficiency. She was like having four assistants in one, they said. A woman heard of this incredible worker and promptly offered Kathleen a job as a receptionist in the garment company where the woman worked.

More adversity. Kathleen now needed a car to get to her new job. Her new salary was not enough to buy even a used car. Inspired by her success so far, Marie and her husband decided to help Kathleen along by offering her their car and buying a new one.

I again suggested to Kathleen that she idealize this new job. At first she used to complain because they asked her to do so many things outside of her job description. I told her she was creating a new career and she had not yet met it. She learned several jobs, including how to choose merchandise for large department stores, inadvertently educating herself as a buyer. A slow season forced the company to lay off several employees. Kathleen by then had become indispensable; she was given a raise and took the place of several people. After a few years she wanted to move back to her hometown, and announced to her company and those she served in other firms that she was leaving. In response she received several offers of work at higher position, including that of buyer, with a salary double to what she was earning. While heartened, she decided to move anyway.

Once at her hometown she was afraid that she would not be able to find work because there was no garment industry there. I suggested that she get letters of recommendation from her old company and from the people who wanted to hire her. These testimonials helped open the door to a brand new career as a manager of a medical clinic.

Many people who have clear ideals do not reach them because they do not want to start from where they are. In my travels I met a man who told me that he was a frustrated writer. He remembered all the legends and stories he was told as a child and felt that the collection would be valuable reading for many generations to come. I agreed and asked him what was so frustrating about writing his book.

"I do not make much money, so I went to all my wealthy relatives and friends. I told them about the book. Everyone thought it was a grand idea. But do you know that not one of those ingrates offered to publish it? This was twenty years ago. I'm still suffering from the betrayal. It is their fault that I did not write my book. And worse, they're not even aware of it."

What they were aware of, I suspect, was this man's professional victimhood. He has the potential of being an author otherwise he would not have even considered it. But he wanted to begin from a higher goal, that of having the money to publish it, rather than to begin his book with the daily and basic task of writing sentences.

I ask all of my students to start a plan that will guide them to their ideals. Creating this plan is the only way to get started. I am always amazed but never shocked at the dramatic impact simply doing this exercise has on my students. There is nothing like coming face-to-face with your future.

Making charts of your ideals is the beginning of a serious commitment with yourself. Putting them on paper works a magic that entices us to take that first step toward our potential. A structure brings order so that we do not have to carry the whole plan around in our head and unscramble it every time we think about it. A chart serves as a contract with oneself and reminds us that we are responsible for creating our destiny.

People sometimes ask, "But what if my ideals change?" That is wonderful, I answer, because discovering your potential may bring you to crossroads where you suddenly see a more exciting possibility. The time and effort spent on your first ideal are never wasted because the learning process and the strength developed bring you to the next ideal.

Goals are subject to change, and unexpected tasks are always revealing themselves as the next opportunity to complete the modified goal. Because one of my first ideals was to create a correspondence course, my task of the day was to contact paper companies to research costs. The person who answered the telephone on my first call was impatient with my lack of knowledge. He made a disrespectful remark and told me he had no time to waste on unintelligent (that is not the word he used) questions and to go find something else to do. I also had my parallel ideal to develop my strength of character and an opportunity to do a task toward it. I took it.

"I am a serious client, and your company offers some of the finest paper made, so if you are so kind, please find me a well mannered salesman. I will wait," I said.

"I'm the president of this company," he screamed, and I could hear him banging his hand on his desk. My instinct was to offer my condolences to his company, but I refrained.

"Please find me a well-mannered salesman, and I will wait," I repeated. He calmed down, asked for my telephone number and called back in minutes. He respectfully gave me all the information I had requested. The costs and the responsibilities incurred on a correspondence course were more than I wanted to commit because I would have had to give up teaching and speaking. That is when I seriously began thinking about this book.

MORAL IDEALS

THE POTENTIAL FOR each of us is to be the highest caliber individual we can imagine. We can choose the virtues we want to develop for our moral vehicle and thereby complement the ideals of our mental vehicle. You can list them as honesty, courage, gentleness, self-confidence and responsibility, or take one of these elements as the ideal and break it down to the values required to meet it, listing them as goals.

Virtues	Goals	Tasks
"I am . . . "	"I want to . . . "	"I must . . . "
Responsible	Improve myself	Do my Five Acts every day
Honest	Speak up more often	Practice by myself
Courageous	Excersise more	Take a walk tonight
Grateful	Have a social life	Call friends
Generous	Become more cultivated	Go to library, opera, plays
	Develop more interests	Call ballet studios

Another prime list may lead with self-expression, an unbreakable spirit, generosity, consistency, intelligence and compassion. It really does not matter which you list as the ideal virtues because they are all related, and in brilliance they all become one.

Suppose we want to develop leadership as an ideal. If we make a list of the high qualities an inspirational leader must have, we will discover quickly that they are the same things that would make us the most elevated human being that we can be. Our first list of priorities might include goals like organizational ability, decisiveness, helpfulness, clarity in communication and grace under pressure. Grace then could be taken as a more immediate ideal, so we would put together a second list of qualities that could include calm and concern for others as main goals. We could make an additional list for bravery, which might include concern for others. Continuing with lists of qualities that go into the making of a leader, we will invariably see how responsibility is connected to decisiveness, helpfulness and so on with other qualities, the attributes of one entwining with the attributes of all the others. The Tom Hanks character in the movie *Saving Private Ryan* was exemplary as much for his love of his men as his hatred of war.

You do not have to be in the military, be elected to govern or head a corporation to strive for the ideals embodied in leadership. You become a leader when your example evokes respect and one person asks you for your opinion. The most powerful and inspiring tool of leadership is giving a good example. It is not necessary to be in the public eye or to earn a massive salary to be in a position of leadership. For example, being a mother is a demanding service of the mental vehicle, and the essence of the woman behind the mother is the moral. Working on both strengthens and expands a woman's potential so that she can continue to grow in a paid occupation or in a talent or interest once her active mothering is over. Indeed, fathers and children also need to be working on both vehicles. To live a vital and healthy life, everyone needs to have two ideals, the mental and the moral, and work on them simultaneously.

LIFE'S BIG IDEA

SOME PEOPLE DO not like what they do for a living, but as we have seen, any job can provide the circumstances in which they grow into a new opportunity. It also pays the bills.

Gerald came to see me for the most common reason that people are attracted to my work. He was stuck. He was by nature a highly disciplined man, and a couple of hours of information and some homework put him back on track. For as far back as he could remember, Gerald's ideal mental gift was to be a classical musician, but his affluent parents wanted him to follow the family tradition and become a lawyer. His heart's desire stayed alive, and in his teens he began to apprentice secretly with a friend who was studying the piano. After high school he submitted to his parent's wishes and entered university to study law. On the day of his graduation he turned over his diploma to his mother and immediately left for Europe to continue his musical education. He made a name there and returned to the United States to seek other opportunities to fulfill his ideal.

I met Gerald at a difficult time in his life when he thought he could go no further. He could not make the rent payments on the house or the piano. He could not buy food or pay bills. He had composed one third of a violin concerto but had writer's block. He sat at the piano at 7:00 A.M. to compose, but was physically weak and too worried to concentrate, so all he did was brood and listen to his growling stomach. Clearly, he needed income, so I asked what kind of work he could do to support himself and his art. He said that he was a man of principle and that he would not write other kinds of music because he felt he would prostitute himself.

In the past he had supported himself writing music for Las Vegas acts and for television shows. He had given it up when he began to write his concerto, but now he realized that being penniless was worse. He came to understand that committing to an ideal means doing whatever needs to be done to stay with it. He saw that writing music other than classical was in fact a blessing because it provided a support system for what he wanted to do. Then he organized his time to make sure that both his income and his classical composing were taken care of. Often we do not see the next step because it is not the one we wish to take. He is now recognized as a serious talent in the world of classical music, and in no small part it is due to his becoming serious about paying his bills and eating regularly.

IT IS NEVER TOO LATE

SOME PEOPLE BLOOM in their early years; others, in their middle years; and some come to full potential in their later years. Grandma Moses began painting after the age of seventy and continued successfully after she was a hundred. Any time is a good time to begin realizing an ideal. My youngest student to date was eight-years-old and my oldest was eighty-six.

Several years ago when I was lecturing in another country, I met Mrs. Montoya who was seventy-five. Although she had gone only to the second grade, she put her five sons through university. Three years before we met, Mrs. Montoya's husband died. She closed up their house, dressed in the black mourning clothes of her culture and moved in with her daughter to await her own death. When four of her sons were about to take a seminar with me, I met Mrs. Montoya at the introductory session. I invited her to join us in the seminar. Reticent because she could barely write, she accepted on the condition that I take notes for her. I agreed. She listened intently and from time to time would nod her head, give me a sweet smile and point at the notebook in front of me. She was always on time and worked very hard on improving herself. The discipline that she built throughout her life made her an ideal student.

At our penultimate class she was not there. Her sons did not know where she was, and as time passed, we all became concerned. Mrs. Montoya arrived one hour late, breathless and excited. She had gone back to her old house, brought in a cleaning crew, painters and gardeners with new plants. A seamstress had arrived with fashion magazines and left with an order for several dresses, all in soft pastels.

"Five acts of improvement a day," Mrs. Montoya explained to me, "were not enough. I am old so I have to catch up." She was doing at least fifteen acts of improvement a day. She wanted to grow as much as she could while we were working together for she feared that she would falter without my encouragement.

I have seldom seen anyone change so fast, but I cannot accept credit for her success. People grow because of their efforts, not mine. Reaching for one's potential is an individual and solitary experience.

Two days later as I completed my check-in at the airport, Mrs. Montoya hurried toward me. She looked very pretty in a peach-colored dress, for which she must have pressed her seamstress very hard to finish. She brought me a pair of vases to keep so that I, in her words, would "never forget" her. As if I ever would.

Weeks later I spoke to several of my students from her group, and they told me that Mrs. Montoya was now the star of her social crowd, sought after for her opinion and advice. As an acknowledged leader, she was the program director, organizing activities like field trips to keep the group entertained. Senior citizen activity groups were unknown in her country, and they are not common today. She was discovering her potential not only as a leader but also as a social pioneer.

We can ignore the call to live life to the fullest, but it will not leave us alone. The instinct is so powerful that if we are not exploiting our potential we are busy covering it up. We offer excuses for our lack of effort or pretend that our dreams are so lofty as to be beyond our capacities, giving us ready-made reasons for always falling short. When people resign to the belief that it is too late to do anything about their potential, they go into mourning. The dullness in their eyes reflects the hopelessness of an empty existence. When I see this look in the eyes of young people, it scares me because their age gives them more energy and less discernment, making them easy prey to corruption and self-destruction. It is sad to see a twenty-year-old grieving for having wasted three or four years in laziness and dissipation, and believing that it is too late to do anything with his life. With fewer and fewer opportunities becoming manifest, to start again seems insurmountable. Even to one so young.

DOING VS. COVETING

A DREAM BECOMES an ideal when we begin to take action on it on a daily basis. If there is no activity, there is no ideal. An ideal demands that we do what needs to be done and keep doing it. To expect to meet a great opportunity, we have to increase our care in little acts so that we prepare for the circumstances we are creating. If we want to meet our opportunities faster, we have to speed our growth and increase the number of daily tasks. We build faith on the proof of our accomplishment.

The need for recognition of our accomplishments is natural. The perverse manifestation of this need is evident in the graffiti all over our cities. It is the only way that many underdeveloped youths have of getting their names read by others. They have no contribution to make, but the instinct to seek recognition is still there.

To seek riches or fame to flatter the ego is far from an ideal. Some bring to perfection superficial aspects of themselves as if they were ideals. Confusing ideals with vanity, many people envy the accomplishments of others and covet the rewards of their efforts.

We cannot take over others' contributions because they are based on their potential. We can steal someone else's potential only by being that other person, and that is impossible. We cannot offer what others offer.

There is a story in Native American folklore of two Indian chiefs and their respective tribes. One lived on top of a cliff and the other at the bottom. The chief at the top could observe those below and saw that they prospered while he and his tribe were deprived of all but the minimum to survive. He watched and watched at all hours to discover the secret. Late one night he got up to watch and saw his counterpart below rubbing a nail between the palms of his hands for a long time. Night after night the chief at the top of the cliff got up to watch the scene below. And night after night he saw the chief rubbing the nail between the palms of his hands. Slowly, methodically, the nail was coddled like a precious stone. So the chief on the hill came to the conclusion that the nail must be magic and that it was the reason for the lower tribe's success. One night he waited to see where the chief hid the nail, and early the next morning the covetous chief met with his warriors to plan the attack that would make the magic nail their own.

Late the next evening they stormed the lower tribe's village and confiscated the nail. It was a horrible battle, and the chief of the lower tribe was killed. The victorious warriors returned to their mountaintop village to use the nail to gain riches and success.

Nothing happened. The nail had no magic power. The chief at the bottom of the cliff used the nail only to rub while he meditated on how to help his people.

When someone else is successful, the more aggressive dreamers imagine that they can do what that person is doing and do it even better. They believe they can take it over and do it efficiently without the effort that it took to create what they covet. If they are successful in appropriating it, they get rid of the creator as soon as possible. Almost a hundred percent of the time they cannot sustain what they usurped, and it begins to die. The usurper's arrogance is usually so strong that he has no qualms about expressing his wants as a serious proposition. He sees it as his ideal. A simple warning for you: successful creative people, no matter their level of growth, always have predators stalking them.

I met several masters in the arts who told me about taking disciples into their fold. They choose to work with students who show some talent and already have a developed sense of ethics. Because of the latter, the disciples are authentic, grateful and hungry to learn. The masters also describe opportunists who could not or would not adhere to the discipline of the truly dedicated and who hid their greed for taking over as well as they could.

One composer trained a promising student to assist him. The student's effort relieved the master of some of the unexciting elements of the master's work. Impatient for his own recognition, the student wanted what he called more opportunity. The composer asked exactly what he meant by that. The student answered that his mentor should retire and turn over all his business to him. The master refused, and the student never spoke to him again.

Sometimes the opportunists are the people in charge. Carlos was a mid-level executive for a company in Latin America. He had been with the company almost from its inception, knew the overall business, could substitute for anyone in an emergency and was diligent in carrying out the responsibilities assigned to him. He trained executives who came to the company from the outside to fill much higher positions than his. For many years Carlos hoped for a promotion. His hopes would soar whenever there was a higher opening then crash when requested to train someone new for that position.

By his forties he felt betrayed, hated the company, blamed it for his circumstances and was in earnest about changing them. His zest helped inspire other students in the class I was teaching to move forward a little faster with their concerns. Carlos took his Five Acts of Improvement a day as only the start of a marathon that strengthened his internal fortitude. His physical demeanor noticeably changed in less than two weeks. His back straightened; his eyes sparkled with new alertness; and his voice took on a more commanding tone.

He made an appointment with his higher ups to present his case in a professional manner. He stated how knowledgeable he was and how strongly he believed he could handle the greater responsibility of a higher position. He came to the meeting with lists of all that he had done in his job and all that he did for the company outside of the job's description, a track record of outstanding service over many years.

His superiors knew him as an efficient employee, but they also knew him as a weak and submissive man. They thought he had no place to go except to a lesser opportunity at another company. Satisfied with the status quo, Carlos' bosses turned down his request for a promotion. They were surprised when he announced that he would quit, and they suggested time to reconsider. With his new unyielding spirit Carlos surprised them further by making his resignation effective immediately.

Excited with his potential, Carlos started his own company. Within three months it was clear that he was becoming a competitive threat to the old company, which unwittingly supplied a stream of disgruntled employees who wanted to work for Carlos. Losing well-trained employees was not the only problem for the original company. Many large accounts refused to work with anyone but Carlos because of his efficient and respectful service. Desperate, his old bosses offered him a part time consulting position at nearly the full time salary that he had earned before he left. Carlos refused. They offered him a new position with higher pay and a title commensurate with his value.

The offer was so attractive, Carlos accepted with some conditions. All of the employees who had gone to work for him were to be rehired as part of his team and with appropriate raises. The manner in which he spoke up for himself left no doubt in anyone's mind that Carlos knew who he was and was not to be pushed around anymore. He received the recognition and respect that were long overdue.

Carlos confided to me later that he was secretly relieved. Building his own company had been grueling, he said, taking up every minute of the day and filling his nights with worry. It prepared him for new leadership responsibilities at the old company, and he would have continued with his business if he had to, but he preferred the relative security of working for others.

Each person reaches a degree of potential according to his state of growth at the moment. An ideal is individual. We have to seek it alone. We cannot expect approval or support from others. If they encourage us, we can be grateful, but our growth does not depend on what anyone else is doing or saying. Neither can we blame anyone if we are unable to fulfill our expectations.

THE CHANGES THAT MATTER

WHEN YOU HAVE your ideals in order, your energy is that of someone living a full, vibrant and decisive life. Even if people do not tell you what they see, you will know it by their reactions to your new way of living and being. You will receive greater demonstrations of respect and admiration. Some people may be fascinated with those who live with ideals, if only for the secret wish to watch them fall.

If we are loyal to our ideals, and responsible in the daily tasks that support them, we will meet our potential. Now is the time to identify your ideals. Only you know your passion. And only you will know the devastation of not succeeding.

1. For your moral vehicle list all the virtues you want to espouse.

2. For your mental vehicle write down the skills and knowledge you want to have, what you want to change and what you want your contribution to the world to be.

CHAPTER 7

The Twin Towers
of Strength

*Heavyweight Vision Requires Heavyweight Character • Three Types of
Decisions • The Big Fear • Respecting Our Word • The Need To
Be Specific • The Strength of Our Language • Increasing the
Value of Our Ideals • The One Escape Clause*

HOW MANY TIMES have you participated in a conversation like this?

"Hello, Linda, let's get together for lunch soon."

"That would be nice. When?"

"I'll call you."

"All right, John. When will you call?"

"Next week sometime."

"When?"

"At the beginning of the week. Monday...no, maybe Tuesday is better."

"Tuesday then?"

"I guess."

"What time will you call?"

"Uh, the morning?"

"What time?"

"Oh, ten or ten-thirty."

"Great, I look forward to speaking with you before eleven on Tuesday."

It seems that making a lunch appointment would be a simple task. But most of us, with our inventory of bad habits collected throughout the years, have become casual with our commitments, breaking them at our convenience. Our words have no power with others or ourselves. Some people hear themselves making promises and suddenly realize they do not intend to keep them. Others recognize this weakness and act accordingly. We not only close doors to opportunities but also open the gates for others to take advantage of us.

Indecisiveness is incapable of supporting great aspirations, and our ambitions become severely limited. No one likes the indecisive, not even the indecisive.

A student of mine named Shirley was in love with a man who had two girlfriends, she being one of them. He was not discreet about either woman, and was amused and flattered by the jealousies he provoked. The rivals competed fiercely with each other, and each hoped to win by default due to the elimination of the other. The triangle had been in a stalemate for years, and the longer each woman competed, the greater her resentment and rage toward the other grew. Then Shirley gave the man an ultimatum: commit only to her or she would withdraw immediately. With magnificent drama the boyfriend said he would retreat to the mountains to meditate on his decision.

I met Shirley a few days before the retreat, and had a long conversation about her sense of dignity and the high cost she was paying in humiliation for this man's love. I told her that a decent person would never place a loved one in such a degrading position as her boyfriend had done to her. He clearly had no fundamental respect for the women or for himself. I then told her the fable of the farmer and the ass.

To simplify his chore of feeding a donkey, a farmer set two bales of hay at opposite ends of his farm. The donkey could not make up its mind which to eat first. It would walk toward one, turn to look at the other and walk back to that one. The closer it got, the more it wanted the other. Back and forth it plodded until it dropped in exhaustion and starved to death between the two bales of hay.

Shirley's face turned deep red from mortification. She made a fast and firm decision to break the relationship with the philandering boyfriend. She took away, as it were, her bale of hay. With Shirley out of the picture the other woman was not interesting to the boyfriend, and he broke off with her.

Soon thereafter the man came to see me. "I'm so unhappy," he began.

"You? But you are the one who humiliated both of those women."

"That was their choice. It was kind of exciting to have them hate each other because of me. Now my whole life feels crummy. I used to be important."

So, you see, another ass collapsed because of one woman's decision.

Most people have difficulty being decisive, not because they are weak, but because they lack the clarity to make distinctions. Some people are capable of making distinctions but are indecisive because they want opposite and conflicting outcomes. And others know what they want but lack the strength to pursue their desires.

Unless we learn to make decisions properly, we will stop at new barriers and always be afraid to take risks. Risk-taking demands clarity and determination, not audacity as is often supposed. We cannot reach certain levels of growth without the support of determined vision that requires decision-making on a daily basis.

HEAVYWEIGHT VISION REQUIRES
HEAVYWEIGHT CHARACTER

REVEREND TIM STOREY of the Tim Storey Ministries in Los Angeles put it best when he said, "Many of us are visionary heavyweights and character lightweights," to describe the notion that people want what they are not willing to build the endurance to achieve.

Just as we must exercise our bodies daily for physical strength and energy, so must we exercise our mind to make choices that support our ideals. An awareness of how we make our small choices of the day is essential to develop the endurance to make intelligent decisions quickly every time. Small choices made well prepare us for the more complicated decisions that will come.

People who do not develop decisiveness often live with the belief that they are doomed to a life of unintelligent decisions and failure. They begin to suspect that something is wrong with them, and ignorant of their gifts, they are irresponsible for their own development. People make significant decisions without thinking and often ruin their lives, causing damage to others and negatively affecting the environment of everyone around them.

THREE TYPES OF DECISIONS

DECISIONS AND COMMITMENTS are our character's twin towers of strength. A harmonious life of success and happiness is the result of clear and firm decisions and the determination to complete them.

There are three types of decisions, and each merits its own approach. The first two require clarity as their basis; the third requires absolute mediocrity. Within these three you will find the procedure for every decision you have ever made and every decision you are yet to make.

1. **Simple decisions** are the little things that we choose everyday in our routine or in slight variations of that routine. Simple decisions are deciding when to take a shower, what to wear, where to sit, what to eat and drink, what time to go to bed and what time to get up. We make hundreds if not thousands of simple decisions every day. Simple decisions must be made quickly and the alternatives dismissed immediately. Simple decisions become complicated by disorder, as in the difficulty of choosing what to wear when our closet is in disarray or misplacing a bill or a letter because we do not use the specific places assigned to them. Taking too long to make simple decisions means our mind is filled with chatter and clutter. There is brilliance in making quick and firm decisions, and dullness in wasting time and delaying others while we linger on a small choice.

   Because a decision is simple does not make it unimportant. Our simple decisions are our daily acts of improvement. These decisions must always be made intelligently, driven by a larger goal and improved constantly. Taking care of the small things at the time they need to be done sharpens the mind and develops efficiency.

2. **Complex decisions** are the big choices that will affect our lives in long term ways. These might include starting or ending a relationship, having children, choosing or changing careers, going back to school, taking a trip, making a large expenditure or moving. Complex decisions always involve advantages and disadvantages that have to be considered together. This whole view insures that we can properly weigh all the consequences simultaneously. The cost of our decision, whether it is money, time, energy or emotional wear and tear, must be studied intently so that we can discern if the price is worthy of the advantages. Complex decisions always carry a sacrifice. Whenever we go after the big idea of our ideals, we always give up something that is important or comfortable. Whatever we decide, we must finally face the fact that we will be under some stress.

3. **Default decisions** can be the most harmful. The attitude of not making a decision produces most of our negative consequences. Not checking the car's engine can lead to being stranded on the freeway, not getting an annual physical can lead to long term health problems and not taking responsibility for your own ideals can leave you old and regretful.

All of the decisions we make represent our way of thinking and maintain the course of our life. The big ones establish defined goals toward our ideals. The small ones build the succession that makes those goals real. The default decisions build the roadblocks. It is imperative to always be aware of our ideals and let them influence our decisions. Significant decisions and choices made lightly will diminish our ideals and totally change the direction of our lives.

The thought of making complex decisions is scary. But making them is freeing.

THE BIG FEAR

ALL BIG DECISIONS must be made in an atmosphere of peace. Create a quiet and orderly place where you find it easy to think clearly. Clear your mind of all clutter so that you can focus on one thing—your Big Decision.

Now take a sheet of paper and fold it in half to create two columns. Across the top write the decision that needs to be made. For example, "Should I buy a new car or keep the old one that is paid for?" In one column write the pros; in the other write the cons.

Should I Buy a New Car or Or Keep the Old One That Is Paid For?

PROS	CONS
Safe and gas efficient	Payments may be difficult to maintain
Compact for easier parking	
Reduce major repair expenses	Payments will reduce disposable income, quality of life
Save time with less down time	
Peace of mind, family safety	Increased insurance and registration costs
Payments may be incentive to raise income	
	No garage to park car properly

This is a very old exercise done in self-help seminars around the world. You probably already know that this exercise helps to reveal all the options available.

What I have found is that no one wants to tell you the awful and awesome truth. No matter what you decide, you will experience anxiety. No amount of lists will change that. We all know the individual who can spend decades wallpapering his house with the pros and cons about moving to a new neighborhood.

What if the list is about love? Marriage? Divorce? What if the list is about changing careers? What if the list is about your pioneering something you have never done before?

What if you are asking "What if?" ten years from now?

Pro or con, we will often meet anxiety no matter what our decision. What prevents us from breaking through it is fear. Yes, there is fear of the unknown. Yes, there is fear of discomfort. But the main fear is that we will not keep our word.

RESPECTING OUR WORD

A COMMITMENT IS an agreement that we make with others or ourselves with a time frame for completion. It is binding. An agreement without a set deadline is a casual comment, not a commitment. Ultimately, a commitment is a guarantee that action will be taken. We have stood on the cons and will not be moved. We have taken the pros and pushed through to completion.

Commitment determines the value and strength of our decision and creates the foundation for self-trust. If we respect our commitments, we develop a sense of honor for our word so deep that we will never have to say, "I give you my word of honor," or, "Trust me." When we respect our word, saying we are going to do something will be so powerful a motivation that we will do it just because we said we would. Our respect for our word is our power. It compels us to stay with our decisions.

Mark, a young man in one of my classes, responded to that comment with a hearty, "I can attest to that." He said that when he was seventeen he worked at a fast food restaurant. In his youth and bravado he repeatedly told everyone who would listen that if he was ever held up he would fight the robber and take away his gun. Mark's co-workers would sometimes chide him about such dangerous intervention. But he was adamant.

One night while he and his co-workers were standing in the restaurant with a gun pointed at them, Mark was amazed at what went through his mind. "For so many years," he thought, "I have promised I would fight, so now I must. If I don't, how can I ever look my friends in the face?" Mark pounced on the criminal causing him to run from the restaurant faster than he had come in. While reckless pride is never enough reason to keep a commitment that could cost your life, the value of Mark's word was firmly established.

THE NEED TO BE SPECIFIC

IF WE ARE casual with our commitments, we are also casual in the manner in which we express ourselves. There is a big difference between the vagueness of "I have to do something" and "I am going to make that call by eleven o'clock." The first gives us license to postpone it; the second compels us to complete it. Commitments are definite, and keeping them tells the world that we take ourselves seriously.

Craig, a former student, was disappointed and angry with his girlfriend because she casually made and broke most of her commitments to him. They would argue often, and she ended every argument with the same phrase: "I am spontaneous, and you are rigid." He loved her regardless and had decided to ask her to marry him. His resentment kept getting in the way, though, as she continued to break dates and keep him waiting interminably when she did make herself available.

I asked Craig to use this situation to practice his decision-making list of pros and cons to see what amount of stress he was willing to live with. His list started with the question "Should I marry this woman?" Under cons he put: she's difficult, irresponsible and unappreciative. Under pros: she is pretty, active and ambitious. Craig retained his original position: yes, he would ask her to marry him.

But Craig wanted his marriage to be one in which commitments were taken seriously. He knew that he could not ask for what he did not first offer, so he vowed to himself to keep his word at all times. By committing to improve himself, he would learn what values his girlfriend, or anyone else, demonstrated toward him. She loved this because he was so reliable.

Craig warned his girlfriend that he would no longer accept her broken commitments. From now on he would wait fifteen minutes and leave if she was not ready. She became very angry and called his new behavior "militaristic impositions" on her free spirit. Craig refused to budge, and instead increased his kindness and consideration for her. She made a few attempts to meet him on time but was seldom successful. During a rare harmonious evening, Craig asked his oft-late girlfriend to marry him. He was shocked at her answer. "You are trying to change me," she said. "You either accept my free spirit and not complain anymore or you can forget marriage. Until you change, the answer is no!"

She then presented Craig her conditions for them to even continue their romance. She was to be permitted to do whatever occurred to her at the moment, and he must accept it just like he used to. "I want our old relationship back," she said. "I was happy then." It made no difference to her that her boyfriend was miserable. He would not compromise and broke up with her.

The stress caused by that decision had Craig coming back to class in a very dark mood. "This does not work," he said. "You said that if I became very precise with my language and acts that she would become defined with me. I asked her to marry me, but she insisted that I let her do whatever she wanted. I couldn't live in a marriage like that and still call myself a man."

"I did not promise you that she would marry you. I promised that she would become defined with you, and she has. She told you exactly what she is willing to offer you and what she will not do for you."

A few months later he was still devastated about the loss of the relationship. But when the girl wanted to get back together under her previous conditions, he refused to go back on his word. Even though he was hurting, he realized the pain of humiliation was worse than the pain of loss. He was committed to strengthening his moral vehicle by working through his pain.

THE STRENGTH OF OUR LANGUAGE

IF WE ARE vague, we can hear it in our language. The following phrases are common, and in the parenthesis are the hypothetical ideals and goals that will never be accomplished.

"Someday I will.....(write a script)."

"I really want to.....(learn Italian)."

"Let's get together soon.....(to discuss that business idea)."

"Maybe I should.....(lose some weight)."

"I'll try, but.....(I will never stop swearing)."

"We really need to…..(build more intimacy)."

The saddest thing about being vague is all the wonderful things in life we choose not to experience. If our commitments are meaningless, our lives will be less abundant. That is why I tell my students to pick some small tasks that they are very uncomfortable with and commit to them as part of their Five Acts of Improvement. You will learn quickly how valuable your word is to you.

Vagueness and mediocrity are part of the same cluster. If we are a serial commitment breaker, we develop an attitude of casualness and familiarity. The vague, undefined in their language and the way they treat others, are never happy with the way they are perceived. They wonder why people do not react positively to the carefully polished image they have created for themselves. They complain that people do not take them seriously and become resentful. Casualness and ambivalence are weaknesses. Our attitude toward our commitments establishes who we are, our level of growth and the value of what we give.

INCREASING THE VALUE OF OUR IDEALS

DECISIVENESS AND COMMITMENT are essential contributors for our journey to mental and moral brilliance. We need them both when we raise our ideals to new levels. They are the foundation of self-acceptance, reliance, strength and courage. They create clarity and action, promise and results. They support our truths and define our soul.

When our word alone is enough to assure that our contracts will be accomplished, we have established one of our first visible strengths. Understanding the power generated by commitments is the next major step in bringing them to fruition. Our commitment is the action, energy and life for our list of ideals. Without this energy our ideals, the big ideas of our soul, are reduced in value.

Decisiveness builds power, confidence, composure and definition. When we are defined, we force others to be defined with us. If we give ourselves a deadline for everything we say we are going to do, it becomes necessary to consistently demand respectful treatment from others. Nailing down the particulars with someone who speaks casually may make that person uncomfortable at first, but if we are to be committed, vagueness is never acceptable. Remember the dialogue at the beginning of this chapter about the lunch date?

It is possible that the call John promises to make will not be made, which means he really had no intention of going to lunch. He was just making small talk. Linda defined herself by demanding a set time from him. He cannot pretend to make a false appointment with her again. The precision of her self-expression will either coerce or inspire him to respect his commitment or stop wasting her time if they meet again. He will either refine his conduct or he will disappear for good. This is just one way self-definition protects us against manipulations both great and small.

In business precision is critical, or you will likely be taken advantage of. Ask business associates what they offer, and you often hear all encompassing but vague answers such as, "I will do whatever you want," or, "I do whatever it takes to get the job done." While these are often said out of eagerness to please, they represent a weakness of character that will affect the quality of your work, your mental vehicle. Now that you are informed, make the necessary adjustments to protect your interests.

Usually the vague are vague only in reference to what they offer, but they are precise with what they expect from you. Some people sign contracts and still attempt to be dishonest about conditions they agreed to. You cannot defend against a liar. I have seen the greedy fight for "their rights" and deny receiving documents, and even accuse others of forging faxes and letters. A nearly infallible rule of thumb for detecting predators is this: They are the ones demanding your precision but never giving it in return.

THE ONE ESCAPE CLAUSE

COMMITMENTS EITHER TO others or to ourselves should be thought of as giving our word of honor. This may sound a little shocking at first, but there is solid precedent for breaking what we honor. Not one of us would enter into a binding pact if we thought we would be betrayed. If we did remain in such an untenable situation, we would be honoring betrayal, not the ideal of keeping our word. We would be honoring what we used to be—unwary or uniformed, immature or silly, fearful or submissive—not the stronger, nobler person we are becoming.

There should be a sense of relief in knowing that the ideal of commitment demands that we walk away from anything that we discover is foolish or abusive, including an earlier destructive agreement. For many, however, the weakness of putting up with things is so pervasive, it takes courage to even look to see if that might be happening. Consider a man who is in partnership with his brother and then discovers the brother has a taste for laziness or fraud . . . Or think about the woman who is married to a second husband whom she discovers . . . Or perhaps you have made a vow when you were alone in the darkness of the night, a vow you thought was to God, but now you wonder if it was really to the false gods called Fear, Used To Be or Wish It Was. It takes tremendous courage to commit to seeking information we may not like. It takes more courage to then declare precisely another way for ourselves. And still more to commit to the brighter path.

But what freedom!

A very timid girl named Marina was asked by a very manipulative cousin named Esther to be the maid-of-honor at Esther's wedding. Marina's yes meant committing to buy the standard ugly-issue dress and matching shoes that Esther had picked out. Then Esther announced that she expected each member of the wedding party, all thirty bridesmaids and groomsmen, to contribute $150 to the cost of the reception. Marina was dumbfounded. Her silence and the silence of the others were taken as agreement because silence makes one an accomplice.

Marina believed in traditional family values and for years had interpreted one of those values as keeping the peace at all costs, even when being walked upon. But the exercises she did from my classes were beginning to awaken something. She hesitantly began to touch what it was by saying that she felt tricked. I asked Marina if she would collect money for her own wedding.

"Of course not," she replied.

"Why?"

"If I couldn't afford a big wedding, I would have a simple, small ceremony."

"Why?"

"I wasn't raised that way. It's not right to ask people to pay for what I can't."

"Why?"

"Well, it's the principle, isn't it?"

"All right. Perhaps there is another way of saying that Esther wants $150 from you."

Marina gave a start. "She wants me to break my principles."

"Is that what you have committed yourself to?"

Marina did not like making the phone call in which she told Esther that she would not contribute the desired money. Marina's marshalling her courage might have ended this story here, but Esther was very cunning. She asked Marina to please announce her decision to the wedding party when it gathered again for a planning meeting. Marina gave a reluctant yes and felt as if she had been tricked one more time. As she mulled over why, Marina realized that she was allowing herself to be cornered. The public announcement was supposed to trap her into declaring herself a pauper or a cheapskate, or if she talked about principles, she could be labeled self-righteous. Undoubtedly the cousin thought that Marina's embarrassment and fear of being an outcast would keep Marina silent and force her to pay the money.

"Principles are exactly why you should speak up," I recommended. "Tell the group the same things you told me. Stand up and request to speak before anyone else."

"And then what?" Marina asked in a small voice.

"Sit comfortably and watch the fireworks."

Within a minute of the start of the meeting, a very uncomfortable Marina had said all she needed to say. There was stunned silence. She took her seat and wished she were somewhere else. Then one by one the other members of the wedding party stood and said they would not be paying $150 either. In fact, they wanted to withdraw from any further participation in the wedding.

Esther began to sob and begged, "Please, what if you just put in fifty?"

No. Thirty times no.

It was not a pretty scene for Esther. But the decisiveness and commitment of one very timid girl unlocked the truth for twenty-nine fellow human beings and freed her to continue a brave walk toward brilliance.

I encourage you to continue your brave walk with the following exercises:

- Practice making quick and firm simple decisions.
- Do three sheets of pros and cons for three complex decisions you are facing.
- Use definitive language for what you are going to do and set a time for completion.
- Do not break a commitment unless you respect your reason for doing so.

With the above you will build decisiveness and commitment to be twin towers on the frontier of the soul. They will defend against marauders—irresponsibility, lack of principle, false accusations, doubt and other entrapments. In them strengths will be fortified. From them we will march out renewed, and to them we shall return in triumph. They are the pillars of our peace.

CHAPTER 8

The Rhythm *of* Victory

What Is Discipline? • *Our Natural Code of Behavior* • *How To Develop the Discipline that Reveals Brilliance* • *The Miracles of Positive Discipline*

IN THE LAST two chapters we have learned how to identify our ideals, decide what our tasks and goals will be and how to commit to them as a matter of mental and moral imperatives. These are exciting intellectual exercises for they set the stage for our truth to break forth. From here forward our moral and mental muscles will be strengthened by leaps and bounds that will keep our ideals on course and allow us to experience brilliance today and tomorrow and for the rest of our lives.

WHAT IS DISCIPLINE?

DISCIPINE IS DEFINED as a system of rules and regulations, and as a prevailing disposition or habit of following them. The discipline of brilliance is the constant exercise of free will to advance our ideals with ever-improving results. It is like an automatic pilot for behavior that we complete by habit until it feels like instinct. Despite fears and regardless of failures, discipline can empower a new sequence of acts that raises our lives from stagnation, from the ordinary to the extraordinary, from boredom to constant and courageous achievement.

Discipline can describe the quality that makes a scoundrel or a tyrant succeed, or what makes an obsessive personality so rigid and inflexible. We must interpret between positive and negative discipline. Positive discipline is strong and structured, and simultaneously flexible and vibrant. These combined qualities, like the beat, melody and harmony of music, give solid shape to actions and flowing rhythm to life.

Some people claim they have no discipline, but everyone on earth, the rich, the poor, the leader and the follower, marches to the drumbeat of some form of discipline. It may create rhythms chaotic, negligent or criminal, but it is discipline nonetheless, and its effectiveness is strengthened, weakened or abused daily throughout the years. Consider the con man who must practice very hard to create a false life or an elaborate scheme that is perfectly crafted to steal money and possessions. Think of all he must have—phony credentials, addresses, cover-ups, protection against being double-crossed and on and on. His baroque and sinister existence moves to twisted but effective discipline.

Positive or negative, it is the application of our discipline that creates a beautiful symphony or an act of terrorism, a breakthrough in science or the breakdown of culture.

The type of discipline we display reveals to others who we are and what we stand for. It is a barometer of our brilliance or lack thereof and always a factor in the quality of care we receive from others. If your discipline of speech is such that you do not curse, others are not likely to swear in your presence. If your discipline allows you to exaggerate, omit information and go back on your word, few people will be prone to believe much of what you say.

Obviously, positive discipline is the type needed to build the virtues and qualities to support our ideals. Not so obvious is that the exercise of positive discipline makes us intimate with its strengths and thus much more sensitive to the weaknesses of negative discipline. We begin to see the truth in others and will not be distracted or fooled by the enticements and abuse that result from their negative discipline. The dilemmas in our relationships that muddle our growth often are due to the clash between positive and negative discipline.

Aesop's fable of the toad and the scorpion is a perfect example of what happens when we are not clear about the difference. A toad was preparing to swim across a pond when a scorpion asked if he could hitch a ride on the toad's back. Said the toad, "No. I believe you will sting me."

"Sting you?" the scorpion laughed, "Don't be absurd! If I sting you, we will both drown. Does it make sense that I would do that to you?"

After pondering a moment, the toad agreed to give the scorpion a ride. Halfway across the pond, the scorpion drove his stinger deep into the toad's back. Stunned and dying, the toad managed to gasp, "Why did you do that?"

"Because it is my nature," replied the scorpion.

The object lesson is that the toad was initially more aware of the scorpion's discipline than he was of his own. His own lay somewhere between the poles of negative and positive, in the mediocre zone, and made his thinking fuzzy with doubt. The toad is not alone. Many of us sacrifice intelligence on the altar of mediocre discipline, mainly because it is easy to do what we always do. But we will get stung every time.

OUR NATURAL CODE OF BEHAVIOR

DISCIPLINE IS THE accumulation of our personal habits and rules. Like our very own operations manual, it answers our questions and dilemmas, and describes everything that we are. If we do not like who we are, the solution is to amend sections of the manual that will improve our habits. If we like where we are but are not experiencing brilliance, we must again re-write or add to the manual. The excitement of following the book labeled Brilliance is that it allows us to always create a new section for self-correction.

In Chapter 2 we discussed the three levels of thought— superior, mediocre and inferior. Here we will learn how discipline brings our thoughts to life.

If twenty percent of the population consistently lives with superior thinking, only twenty percent of the actions committed daily around the world are superior. Surprising? Not at all. It explains the great amount of pain and confusion we see all around us.

Thousands of private students have come to see me over the years. With few exceptions the suffering I see in my office is caused by the chasm between what we know we can be and what we really are. The soul is always clear about its ideals and purpose, but for many of us the weakness of our moral and mental vehicles prohibits the long drive to achieve greatness. Any act or habit not fully congruent with the moral and mental vehicles is negative and will create a discordant dance of disappointment and failure.

There is a curious thing about discipline that I have learned from my students and my own life. Sometimes our very strong and gracious discipline is applied full force . . . to the wrong ideals! We work very hard to achieve goals our soul has not asked for. People often ask me if there is an easy way to tell whether the discipline with which they live is misguided, and I believe there is.

You may be living with misguided discipline—discipline that is not continuously growing to meet your ideals—if you are:

- Bored even in activity
- Unfulfilled, watching life from the outside
- Not challenged and never satisfied
- Morally and mentally fatigued
- Hampered by avarice or resentment
- Certain you can do better and contribute more

Most of these circumstances are caused by weakness of character, and we are learning right now how to develop the strength we need to live with the light of brilliance.

Weakness is easier to recognize in its outcome than its actions. The outcomes are universal, and I listed them above. Weakness thrives in the thinking that creates our actions, so to discover the barriers to positive discipline, we must examine the roots of our thoughts and the habits they create.

HOW TO DEVELOP THE DISCIPLINE THAT REVEALS BRILLIANCE

GOD'S GIFT OF free will enables each of us to decide the quality of our life within our given circumstances. Throughout history some of the most unlikely people have risen to shape the world with the power of their minds and the clarity of their ideals. Enormous potential is inherent in everyone, and so is the free will to fail.

There is a passage that I read years ago in Ralph Waldo Emerson's essay *Self-Reliance* that hauntingly describes the grief that can result from not applying positive discipline to our lives: "A man should learn to detect and watch that gleam of light that flashes across his mind from within, more than the luster of the firmament of bards and sages. Yet he dismisses without notice his thought, because it is his. In every work of genius we recognize our own rejected thoughts; they come back to us with a certain alienated majesty." Have you ever seen your own gleam of light surface in the great accomplishments of others?

The first imperative for creating positive discipline requires knowing our ideals and committing to them. The exercises in Chapter 6 and Chapter 7 are designed to make these ideals clear and organic, living not just in our minds but documented on paper or in our computers. Ideas not expressed, even to an audience of one, are lifeless.

The second imperative to creating positive discipline is the recognition of our gifts and talents, and being obedient to their maximum development.

Several years ago I met a mother who had two beautiful daughters. The elder was a natural athlete. By twelve years of age she had trained herself to perform acrobatic feats at an advanced level. Her younger sister was the opposite and would fall down performing even the most rudimentary exercises. Her body language spoke of awkwardness and timidity. I suggested to the mother that she sign the little one up for gym classes at the YMCA. "Oh no," she said. "If one of them takes classes, it

will be the older one because she is the one with all the talent."
The mother, however, did the intelligent thing and enrolled
both daughters.

Three months later the older daughter dropped out of the
course. She believed there was nothing new she could learn.
Meanwhile the little one stayed with the program. She began
to walk in the manner of a gymnast, on the balls of her feet like
a graceful young panther. Within one year she had mastered
her art to such a degree that she was chosen to join a group of
children who had been invited to perform in Australia.

The older sister was truly gifted and a potential star. Her
mental vehicle was strong, but she had parked her moral vehicle. By not caring for her natural gifts and using every opportunity to improve upon her abilities, she set in motion a process
that indicated she would probably not bring them to brilliance.
If we fail to support our mental gifts with moral strength, we
will lose the gifts. Undeveloped gifts do not go away; they
remain in our soul as mutilations.

The third imperative to create positive discipline is to continuously improve our habits day in and day out. Our Five Acts
of Improvement elevate the manner in which we think. Con-
tinual improvement creates new habits of precise thought. A
speed of mind develops that allows us to decipher and consider
our ideas very quickly. Instead of laboring for months, we find
that hours and sometimes minutes will do.

There is an observation game you can do here to support
this point. Pick someone whom you recognize to be living with
superior thinking and take notice of the speed of his or her
actions. Notice the order and efficiency that constant improvement creates. These people are not always losing their keys or
looking for their briefcase or glasses. They do not turn simple

decisions into monologues of doubt and confusion. Notice the sparkle in their eyes and the quickness of their wit. They respect their time and the time of others.

THE MIRACLES OF POSITIVE DISCIPLINE

AS YOU DIRECT your actions with positive discipline, you will experience the following miracles:

We are forever better today than we were yesterday. (It is shocking that this is not inherently true because it seems reasonable that repetition would lead to perfection. But as we discussed, repetition without improvement leads to decline.) We will never again willingly acquiesce to the dullness of mediocrity. Instead we will claim the service and beauty of our soul's calling.

A wonderful and talented student of mine named David had a very successful career as a set designer for Hollywood movies. One day, rather frustrated, he came to me for help. "How will I ever get the experience I need to become a film director?" he asked. "I've always wanted to direct, but I'm afraid I may become stuck where I am."

I love this kind of question! "You must do at least one act a day towards your new career. Start thinking like a director and solving problems like a director."

"But I'm not a director, and the real director may be offended," he said.

"I did not tell you to be the director. Be respectful of authority, but think and contribute as a director would. Do not be concerned if your ideas are not accepted."

He promised to begin this exercise immediately. Five months later I saw David again, and even I was shocked by the ferocity of his momentum.

"There have been some big changes," he began excitedly. "When I began to think like a director, I began to see filmmaking as a whole discipline and to appreciate all the separate talents that create a movie. So then I started to think about what kind of story I would want to direct, and I wrote it. Then I began to think like a producer and began to raise some money to cover the costs. And soon I will become a director of my own film!"

The second miracle to positive discipline is the unveiling of the natural beauty and elegance of our soul. Love and care will envelop all of our actions and create an infectious sense of calm and confidence. We recognize this phenomenon in others. They are the people that we just love to be around. They are the ones who inspire, create laughter and bring serenity. Their smiles are from the heart, and their eyes seem to radiate pure energy. We are on our way to becoming one of these people.

The third miracle is related to the elegance of our soul. We will project a confidence and charisma that is undeniable. No matter how wild a departure from your current life your new ideals may be and how great a leap of faith must be made to march toward them, the simple decision to identify, develop and complete your ideals is life changing. A synergy develops with others who are on a path to brilliance, and our combined efforts gel to create a powerful alliance.

As we move towards brilliance, we reach a place where all of our relationships are refined and promote dignity, happiness and support for people who exhibit their finest ideals.

The fourth and final miracle is the inspiration our actions will provide for others. My own efforts are supported by the lives of people I know and do not know, who have fought, struggled, failed, learned and accomplished their missions. Famous and unknown, young and old, male and female, the achievers of our world always carry those who need assistance and clarity. The brilliance of the Founding Fathers, the bravery of our veterans and the principles of our greatest leaders are all responsible for my ability to write this book. Without freedom, ideas like mine cannot gain acceptance; without fighters our freedom of expression would have been compromised; and without guardians of the Constitution we would be ready prey for the inferior thinkers.

Each act of discipline and each life of brilliance form a thread throughout time that help make the human experience a blessed one. Contribute to the thread by doing the following exercises:

1.   Learn to recognize discipline in the lives of others. This is one of my favorite assignments, and I am always thrilled by the reaction it receives.

      Please select the biography or autobiography of an accomplished person in each of these fields—science, music, business, art, entertainment, politics and religion. Read all of them during the next year. Mix your selection to include at least two books on people with whom you are not at all knowledgeable. You may even include a selection about an infamous subject. Try to span history and include some ancient figures as well as contemporaries.

      From each book identify the qualities that the subject developed as the result of positive discipline. We will discover the same qualities we need to achieve our ideals is constant throughout time.

2.   Learn the consequences of your own discipline. This exercise is simple and fun.

      Make a chart with two columns. In the left column

write one bad habit and no more than two. Complaining, smoking, swearing and tardiness may be examples. In the right column list at least five simple daily pleasures that you cherish—perhaps morning coffee, a glass of Chianti, a special item of clothing or jewelry, or a favorite television program.

Each time you violate the behavior in the left column, you must revoke the top item in the cherished item list for twenty-four hours. After twenty-four hours of not repeating the action (that is twenty-four hours of positive discipline) you may return that item to your list. If you lose all of your simple pleasures for a week or more, you will derive one important benefit, and that is a greater understanding of the need for discipline.

A final and important point. Do not think of your pleasures as rewards for breaking the bad habit. A reward isolates what you have overcome instead of allowing you to enjoy the victory as a natural sequence of living.

CHAPTER 9

The Two-Year-Old Dictator

How We Learn To Think • *Making the Wrong Turn* • *Destiny vs. Fate* • *At the Crossroads*

CHILDREN ALL OVER the world plant beans as a class project, and so it was when I was in second grade. The teacher told us to bring our own pots. My mother painted mine bright red and filled it with black, fertile earth. The teacher went around the classroom and gave each pupil a bean, and we planted them at the same time. Every few days she showed large illustrations that depicted the stages of growth for a bean. When everyone went to recess, I would check my bean to see if it matched the pictures the teacher showed. I took it out of the soil for only a little while, and I quickly put it back exactly where it was supposed to be each time. We did fine, my bean and I, for a while.

Then everyone's pot began to show a little sprout except

mine. The teacher said not to worry. Soon all the other sprouts looked more like little plants, but there still was nothing to be seen in my pot. One day the teacher gave out small sticks so that all the children could wrap their vines around them. My stick was so barren, I felt humiliated. Finally the teacher wondered how it was that my bean had not even sprouted when it came from the same packet as everyone else's. She asked me if I had done anything to it. Oh yes, I replied, and told her how I kept checking my bean's growth with the beautiful pictures.

"That explains it," she said. "It died."

I wondered what killed the bean. Touching it or bringing it into the light. "How did it die?" I asked.

She thought about that for a moment and said, "When you got it into your head to dig up the bean, it was only a matter of time." She gave me another to plant at home, but I did not want to do the project alone, so that bean died too.

Over the years I have met at least a half dozen bean killers who remember digging up their beans as I did. In retrospect I learned several important lessons. The Law of Responsibility indicates that if success does not follow good intent and effort, there is probably data missing. Do not dig up the bean. Because I did not want to plant another on my own, I missed my next opportunity to be successful. Another lesson is that it takes patience to allow things to take root and grow. I discovered that care dissolves doubt. It was my determination to do something—my thought—that was the kiss of death to that bean.

Positive or negative, a determined thought means that a deed is as good as done.

HOW WE LEARN TO THINK

THE ANCIENT GREEKS said that the world belonged to the thinkers, referring to those who live in the superior level of thought. Without the ability to analyze and discern, weigh options and come to viable decisions that we are committed to carry out, we will wander off the path to brilliance into recognizable but painful places, repeating the same mistakes, frustrated by familiar but unlearned lessons.

Whether we are aware of it or not, the universal law of cause and effect inexorably rules us. Sir Isaac Newton advanced the progress of the world when he discovered the Four Laws of Motion, the third of which states that for each action there is an equal and opposite reaction. No exceptions. Newton applied this revelation not to the self, but the principle is exactly the same. If we think in the superior level, we will make intelligent choices. Among the consequences will be the discovery of our life's purpose. Finding our course will cause the blossoming of our potential, and that in turn will open the way to meeting our destiny.

The human animal is a thinking being as soon as his brain is formed. There are pictures of fetuses that suck their thumbs, which means that the tiny hands obeyed a desire or rudimentary thought. Dr. Justin D. Call, a founder in the field of infant psychiatry, noted in the early 1960's that within about three days of birth newborns learn and adapt to their mother's feeding habits and styles. They can tell when feedings are about to occur and can signal by turning and opening their mouths that they were ready. In other words, when we were babies, we thought and understood, perhaps only intuitively, that what we did had consequences.

Even though the infant has no words, action follows

thought, and that sequence will continue throughout his life. As the child grows, his way of thinking will be enriched with learning. Yet his natural and learned facility will most likely remain underdeveloped because very few persons know how to think clearly. The ideal would be to be taught how to think when we are small because the thinking behind the acts we do as children affects every action for the rest of our lives. Our second choice is to learn as soon as the opportunity presents itself.

But before a child can ever make up his mind about learning, he is already being taught. In the chapter on mediocrity we discussed how children learn by copying so that they can adapt to society. Everything is learned by example or by the trial and error of self-effort—to crawl, to speak, to walk, to run and when to stop running, to wash hands and to comb hair. We learn how to read, to write, to work. We learn to take care of ourselves and others, to love and to be loved.

Although children are taught how to do everything needed to fit into the world, there is little or no teaching about discerning why they must do one action and not another. We are told by our parents or authority figures that such-and-such is proper, correct or safe simply because they say so. Usually there is nothing about consequences beyond the repercussions of disobedience. There is almost no mention of motivation, the quality of effort behind our choices or the benefit of improving what we do and who we are. We are not taught the powerful effects these have on our character. Neither are we told that our character dictates the quality of our life. Here lies the source of our victories and our greatest legacy, or the source of our failures and our greatest tragedy. With a weak character as a foundation we become fearful of challenges instead of embracing them as opportunities to grow.

To add discernment and order to our thinking, we need to understand the learning process that we followed from early childhood on. Then we will be able to recognize where we stopped stretching and growing and began to repeat all we did with variations. The influence of authority figures will become evident, and we can shed those patterns of thought that we do not wish to use anymore. Each of us will replace them with his own. Parents give their children the best they have. Not receiving the necessary tools for successful living from our parents does not condemn us to live without them. Nor can we take license and blame others because we can change all those patterns right now.

MAKING THE WRONG TURN

THE AVERAGE ADULT lives with the belief system he established as a two-year-old. During childhood most decisions are made for you. The country you live in, your home and neighborhood, the language you speak, the religion you follow, the school you attend, the doctor and dentist who take care of you, and legions of other choices are made by parents and other authority figures. There are some choices (within parental guidelines) that you can make in your childhood years concerning what to wear, games to play, some favorite foods, friends and the like. But every child makes one major choice. It is the most transcendental decision of his entire life. He makes it at about two years of age.

He accepts as fact his assumption of what he is worth.

No child, no matter how precocious, is equipped to make such an informed evaluation of himself at that stage or at any other of his childhood. But from this early moment on, self-judgment influences his every act. Different pre-school teachers have told me their small charges quickly establish themselves as leaders, bullies and individuals who are detached, indolent or victims. In just a matter of days they all know who speaks up, who are the caring ones, who can be pushed, who cries easily, who is strong and will stand up for his rights, and who is the bully who will usurp rights. All of this in the realm of toddlers! Some will follow leaders and others will submit to bullies.

Based on an immature concept of himself, the adolescent and later the adult builds the foundation for everything he believes. This immature opinion of himself is what he relies upon for his pursuit of happiness. It will limit or encourage what he thinks he can do and how far he can go.

Children arrive at the assumption of their self-worth by interpreting how authority figures react to them. If children feel admired, respected and appreciated, they will form a high opinion of themselves and grow up striving to maintain and surpass the self-image. Without respect and dignity the child will grow into the insecure adult. The self-concept of a child who is not lovingly disciplined, or feels rejected and ignored will manifest in actions that further minimize his life. According to the immature opinion of himself, he may take an isolated value that has not been stifled and apply it to work or service that has not been crushed, but he will ignore improving everything else.

Equally limited are the efforts of a child who is so praised that conceit and vanity make up his damaged self-concept. Full of himself, his belief system tells him that since he is so beautiful, so bright and so charming all he has to do is smile. This child may appear as self-confident, but he is very insecure because everything he does must be perfect on the first try. He will not take risks for fear of making a mistake. The fear is not so much for the imagined mistake but for the disapproval and criticism that he is convinced it will bring. Criticism invalidates his image, so he cannot accept correction. To maintain public opinion is extremely important to him, so he learns quickly to cover, pretend and deceive. As an adult he becomes a charming manipulator.

A child who undergoes constant bruising to the spirit is another one who cannot grow into a healthy adult. Imagine living a great portion of your life barely healing from the last blow. You have only enough strength to stand up before you get struck again. You are never strong enough to be prepared or defend against the next hit, only to be taken advantage of one more time.

Accepting any childhood belief system as fixed positions us as victims. We hold back from every challenge larger than our present strength, and instead of initiative, procrastination becomes our tool for living. We learned at the beginning of the book that postponing solutions forges a chain of consequences that binds us like prisoners. Learning how to think clearly, however, breaks the shackles of false belief.

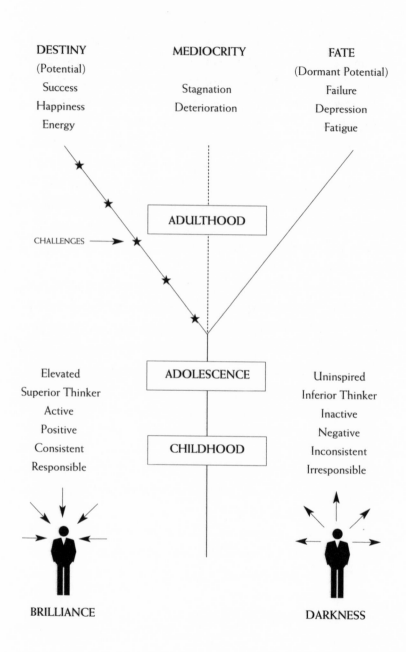

DESTINY VS. FATE

LET US STUDY the diagram at the left to understand the stages of thinking that stunt or nourish the potential within us.

The shape of the Y symbolizes one's life. The stem stands for childhood. The two arms represent two possible directions you can follow through adulthood.

DESTINY is the way of success, and that road is for the thinker who takes both moral and mental vehicles toward perfection. The more you do, the more confident you will be that you will reach your potential.

FATE is the way of failure. It is the road most traveled. You do not have to do much to meet your fate.

The dotted line in the center of the Y represents the middle ground—stagnation—the place of no decisions with all the deterioration that mediocrity entails.

The two figures represent the attitudes behind the results listed on opposite arms of the Y. The arrows pointing toward the figure of brilliance represent the attitude of seeking responsibility in everything that happens to him. After questioning himself about his participation in a situation, he will find the answer and affect an improvement or a solution. The arrows pointing away from the figure in darkness represent the opposite—looking to everyone and everything else as the cause of what is happening to him.

Some of the thinking for either figure must be repetitive, copying examples and accepting them as reliable, then repeating them until they become automatic. This is basic for any training and for any manner of small choices we make as adults.

But the figure in darkness never goes beyond copying. There is no intimate self-examination. No singular values selected as objective, irrefutable ideals. No initiative to take risks from what he has done before. No commitment to find one's true potential.

There comes a moment when such a person thinks he is free to choose a path, usually in regard to a career or an occupation. One says, for example, I will be an engineer or an accountant and follows what he believes is Destiny's path to fulfill that choice. But there is a vast difference between an average professional and a brilliant one.

We have two divergent paths each leading to a place of arrival—Destiny or Fate—one the extreme opposite of the other. Destiny's path proves to us that the concept of our two-year-old was a total misconception and that we are a worthy person. The other path confirms the old beliefs and adds to our confusion and feelings of worthlessness. We must walk one path or the other.

The path to Destiny is a constant facing and overcoming of challenges, leaving nothing unsolved, resting for a while and generating more energy through more action to continue on. It is the way of the free spirit. The way of courage.

The way of cowardice is Fate. It can seem calmer and easier, but that is due to the avoidance of challenges. Situations do not appear unsolved because they are postponed. But there is moral fatigue in this self-indulgence from which there is no rest. To believe that we are on the right path then realize that our journey takes us farther away from our ideals every year is a rude awakening. We find that the Fate we create by omission is much harsher on us than any difficulty faced on the road to Destiny.

Choosing to walk in the way that worked when we were children is the same as refusing to mature and gain wisdom. Parents monitor immaturity in a child to prevent his damaging himself and others. Immaturity in the adult is imprudent and dangerous.

AT THE CROSSROADS

WE CAN EXCUSE the two-year-old for not knowing that he took the wrong direction. But as adults we have no excuses. We can continue to live under the tyranny of our own making, or we can step away to freedom.

CHAPTER 10

The Courage
To Be Brilliant

IN A FAR away forest there was a model beehive renown for its organization and productivity. Every bee is born to do a particular chore throughout life, and the bees in this colony were extremely efficient in their division of labor. Everything was done just so, exactly the same every day.

Among the bees was Beatrice who was in charge of maintaining a section of cells at the bottom of the hive. Bea did her work on the waxen cells to what she thought was perfection. Because she never left the hive, she really had nothing with which to compare her work. However, she knew that she did what she was told and that everyone approved, and therefore she could be proud of the results.

One day a comb from the upper part of the hive, heavy with honey, broke loose and crashed through Bea's section. She panicked. Never had there been such damage. She knew she had to repair her section before the other bees returned or she would be in serious trouble. But, she told herself, if she worked extra hard and extremely fast, then she could tell the story of what had happened, and the other bees would congratulate her on a job well done. Marshalling her resolve, Bea flew toward the hole. As she got closer, the dot of brightness was like nothing she had seen before, and as the ray of light got bigger, she suddenly realized that she could look out of the hive for the first time in her life!

Dare she?

Curiosity got the better of her, and she peeked. The unexpected whiff of fresh mountain air made her dizzy, so much that at first she could not breathe, and the impact of what she saw paralyzed her for a moment. The landscape was beyond imagination. There was so much color—a blue sky, a myriad of greens, flowers of all sizes and shapes, butterflies and birds— and as if that were not enough, there was music in the air. Larks and mocking birds joined their voices to the song of a stream and to the sound of wind roiling through the trees.

Bea forced herself to break the marvelous spell. She began to work diligently on the repairs, thinking all the time, I must finish before they come. I must, I must! What will they say if I do not?

Well, of course, she did finish before the other bees returned. As she initially thought, she told her story, and they all approved that she had done what she had always done, precisely, just as they expected, just as she had been told.

Days went by, and everything continued in the hive as before. Everything except what was going on inside Bea's heart and mind. She could not stop remembering the magic of what she had seen. At times she wondered if she had only imagined it. At other times she wished that she had done her repair work a little less diligently so that there might be just a tiny pinhole from which she could peek out one more time.

After awhile Bea became bored with her work and discontent with having to do it always the same way. She began to dream of going to the magic place outside of the hive where there was so much to see and undoubtedly so many places to visit. She finally came to the point where she could no longer contain herself. She knew that even if the magic was only in her mind she had to fly out of the hive.

And fly she did.

She was seen. It was duly reported that she had escaped under the power of her own two wings. "Such rebellion! How dare she?" the other bees asked. "Who does she think she is? Better than us? Ha! Such nonsense. Where does she think she is going, and what does she think she is going to do once she gets there? That Bea will be in big trouble when she comes back!"

Had Bea died in some catastrophe, the talk would have been about honor and duty, and how Bea was a wonderful example to all who knew her. As it was, there was no news of her for days. The days turned into weeks; the weeks, into months. Common anger turned into false concern: "Poor Bea, she must have failed her crazy aspirations. If she hasn't died, she must be starving. When she comes back defeated and humiliated, we will be noble and forgive her."

More time passed, and when Bea came up in conversation, which was less and less frequently, she was used as a negative example in tones of solemn regret. After a while she was completely forgotten. Not once did any of the thousands of bees in that model hive ever think, I wish she is successful. I hope she makes it. It was beyond any of them to suppose that Bea might have been right because that would mean there was something wrong with the rest of them. And everyone knows that no one is better than anyone else is. We are all the same.

Meanwhile Bea was so excited by the number of choices outside the hive that she did not know what to do. She wanted to see, hear and smell everything. The new experience of freedom had her flying all over the place. Then she realized that she needed to be still for a moment and consider what to do with the rest of her life. She decided that she wanted to build the most exquisite beehive she possibly could. She picked the most beautiful place she could find and began the task all by herself.

Soon other bees were attracted to her energy and joy. They attached themselves to her leadership. Bea responded with increasing confidence, and began to act and look like a queen. The labor and love that Bea and her friends put into the hive stunned them all when they flew back to survey the finished work. As befitting the most perfect hive any of them had ever seen (and now true comparisons could be made), Queen Beatrice ordered that they must collect nectar only from fresh, healthy flowers and that they had to improve their work every day in any way they could. The resulting honey was the best that could be found anywhere. The hive's reputation grew and grew until every creature in the forest had heard of the loving queen, the beautiful hive and the delicious honey.

Thus the fame of Queen Beatrice got back to the first hive, where the old bees said with pride, "She was a sister to us. We taught her everything she knows." Not one remembered being jealous of Bea or sabotaging her reputation. But they remained constant in their belief that everyone is the same. That way they were sure that, given a lucky break like Bea's, they could have achieved exactly the same.

BREAKING FREE

WE ARE ALL like bees confined to a hive until we dare to be different. We dare with the bravest by simply using the wings of our own free will to take flight from mediocrity. It is disconcerting to know that we cannot expect anyone to help, and not many will want us to succeed.

But most of us are our own worst enemy. There is a mistaken consensus that the courage to break free has to do with having no fear, or that courage is some kind of feeling. Courage is all action—taking small purposeful steps from mediocrity regardless of feelings or fear. Too often we refuse to concentrate on what needs to be done. Rather, we seek different steps or more radical ones. They are not there. Our confusion opens us to self-criticism and doubt.

GRAND PASSION COMES FROM
ORDINARY PERSEVERANCE

AT EVERY LEVEL of growth we will experience some irritation, some uncertainty, some negative that we are probably too familiar with already. But now we have the tools to understand what level of thought the negatives come from, and we can label them for what they are—emotions, feelings, mind chatter, past attitudes. They are not ideals. They are not decisive actions. They are not our destiny. We might call them lack of faith or lack of courage or, like Beatrice in the story, only something in our imagination. If we allow them, they can stop us from moving forward. But know this: those negatives are not anything that matters to brilliance. They are the consequences of being trapped in mediocrity. And they scatter like frightened crows before our strength.

Our strength builds with every intelligent action taken from a choice of conviction. Each action, no matter how small, attracts and magnifies the energy dormant in our unseen brilliance. As light comes to light, we see our first results. We like them and respect ourselves for achieving them. As we keep improving our efforts to be our best, step by step the momentum of our growth builds more vitality. More results energize us to greater zeal, less negativity, and our actions, no matter how difficult in the beginning, take on fluidity once unknown to us. We are confident in the way we are thinking. We love what we create from it. We get passionate about brilliance. And because we are passionate, we never want to turn back from the determined steps that march us forward.

Are your steps taking you to the excitement you desire?

PICTURING YOUR LIFE OF
CHARACTER AND GRACE

THINK FOR A moment and ask yourself, What do I really want my life to be like five or ten years from now? Below are some aspects I would like you to consider. For each of them write a short description of what you want. You should do this exercise in light of your new ideals. Be honest with your desires and remember that you can always change them later. Be bold and imagine the best for yourself. Unlike the exercise in Chapter 2 that revealed the bleak fate we might be limping toward, this exercise maps the destiny we can create with continuous and effective use of our moral and mental vehicles.

- Your home
- Your friends
- Your social life

- Your profession
- Your health
- Your spiritual life
- Your family
- Your hobbies and talents
- Your sports
- Your personality
- Your intellect
- Your finances
- Your cultural interests
- Your harmony
- Your character
- Your dignity
- Your contribution to society
- Your charitable donations

Now consider the actions you are presently taking in each area. Will the ways you are driving your moral and mental vehicles get you to where you want to go?

Think about it.

BREAKTHROUGH OR BREAKDOWN

AFTER DOING THIS exercise most of my students suddenly realize that much of the life they are leading will not take them to where they want to go. Some are shocked. Some weep from regret. Some instigate immediate changes. They redouble their Five Acts and apply the lessons in this book more diligently so that they can quickly get on track.

The process of examining what we want helps us to see if we are creating it. A person might consider the family aspect and choose a day in the future, any day, and perhaps list harmony and happiness as two desired elements. Then the question is whether today's actions are the results of intelligent thought and therefore building tomorrow's warmth and well being. Remember that what we have today indicates what we will have in the future.

What do you want in your marriage five years from now? A closer relationship with your spouse? How are you creating that intimacy now?

What kind of friends do you want? Are you cultivating people of caliber? If you are, are you treating them with the respect due to them or are you stabbing them in the back?

Do you want to entertain more and serve delicious gourmet meals? Are you learning how to cook now?

What about that wish to play the piano?

Those thoughts you have had about switching jobs?

What about . . . ?

The blanks are many, and we can all fill them in. This exercise helps conceptualize the future, but if that perfect world is left on paper, on paper is where it will stay. If you want to play golf five years from now, that does not mean that you want to learn the game in the future. It means that you have the motivation to do something now. Start today what you really want to have tomorrow.

WHAT IF YOU CANNOT ENVISION THE FUTURE?

I HAVE BEEN invited on occasion to speak to groups of retired men and to women whose children have left home. Often men die two years after they leave their jobs, and many mothers collapse in depression. Both are effectively retired, and neither has planned beyond retirement. The plans were limited to marriage and family or to a successful career. By the time those plans are fulfilled, there is little motivation to begin anything new.

Some people have in their early plans the study of a career or to advance in one, and over time they find that the career no longer satisfies them, but they are unable to paint a picture of a different future. They cannot even put on paper what would be the elements of a brilliant life. Many of my students start out this way. Depression, confusion and habit blind them from seeing brilliance.

That is the way it was for me.

Before I started this work I had a career in design but wanted something different. I did not know what. I spent many anxious hours thinking about what I could do and might do and should do. All the options were unattractive, and considering them made me more frustrated, more unhappy and more afraid of change. There was only one thing left to do.

I turned to God.

I went into a garden and, without being aware of time, spent two hours in prayer that touched my despair but reached out to hope. I have since shared the gist of my prayer with thousands of students who were stagnant and did not know what to do with their lives. As far as I have been able to document, they all got answers. Even the students who did not believe in God. I will now share that prayer with you, and I invite you to change it to fit the needs of your heart.

PRAYER FOR PURPOSE

LORD, PLEASE LISTEN to the soul of a child who speaks to You. It is I, Your daughter, talking to her Father from the heart.

You said if I asked I would receive. I am at Your feet to make the most important request of my life. I trust Your word, so I expect a gift from You. Help me recognize it and be ready to accept it.

I want an opportunity, a job, a career, or anything You deem would be best for me. I want to develop all of my gifts and strengths to offer as my contribution to this planet. I desire that my contribution be the greatest that I can make. I do not want a mere existence. I want to live and serve. Give me the grace to be grateful and the courage to do my best.

Lord, help me face all my challenges, and help me fight my weaknesses and win.

Help me forgive those who damaged me, and help me forgive myself for any damage I may have caused.

Guide me to the simplicity of my authenticity, Your Truth in me. Take me by the hand and introduce me to the purest and highest being that I can be. Bring out of me the pretty bouquet of virtues whose seeds You planted in me. Make me aware of my growth on a daily basis and let me experience joy as I become more and more aware of Your presence in me. Open Your heart and let me mesh as one with Your light and show me how to share this gift with others.

And when I fail, O Lord, help me to start again. And I will start again as long as You do not take away Your presence.

Thank you, Lord, for listening to me. I expect an answer. I will accept it. And I thank You now for giving it to me.

Amen.

GRACE NOTE

IT WAS TWENTY-FIVE years ago, exactly three weeks to the day after I said the above prayer, when I began this beautiful work that I do. There is no way I could have asked for this in the garden because I did not know that such bounty existed. I started small with only two students. Nothing radical there, but that led to endless opportunities for growth that brought joyful purpose to my life.

It was like the words that my father spoke to me that weekend when I was still new to the title of Master Mopper. I had discovered the dance of life, he said, when I gave everything I had to making sure that the mop would not leave streaks. It was not in the glamour of the activity that I came to that spark of mastery within myself. I discovered it in the most humble activity of my daily life at that time. Mastery is always in the way we do the little things. It is in them that we find the courage to be brilliant.

Acknowledgments

SOMEWHERE IN THE process of teaching and living, my work and I became one. This book represents a great portion of my life. I want to thank those who lived it with me, contributed to it and saw to it that neither the work nor I perished.

First and always to almighty God for answering my prayer with this wonderful opportunity and for the constant care and guidance He provides. *For the word of God is quick, and powerful. . . . (Hebrews 4:12)*.

My late mentor Pilar Garcia-Bailon who taught me how to think and to go beyond my fears.

Vito Sanzone, my publisher, who loves this work as much as I do, and had the courage and vision to bring it to the public.

Jeff Andrus, our writer who jumped into the abyss with this project, for his fine manner and dedication.

To his wife Gwynneth Andrus who allowed us to make an office of her home and fed us into the wee hours of the morning.

My children Oscar, Eileen and Marco Monahan who are close to my heart and have always been present.

The friend of my soul Carmen Mora de Triulzi who always believed in me and who has stood by me in my most painful moments.

My dear close friend Alma Rubinfeld who for many years has supplied me with encouragement on a daily basis.

Yolanda Nava who has been so committed a supporter as to be almost militant.

Susan Schweit, *aka* Susanita, who has shared her hospitality with us and who braved a downpour on the Golden Gate Bridge to get me to a lecture on time.

Barbara Barry who is a brilliant example of what I am trying to teach and is a devoted spokeswoman for this work.

Linda Kleinschmit who is personally responsible for creating a following of hundreds of students.

Rhana Pytell whose personal courage in her own life and support of my work has been inspirational to me.

Mark Young who held our hands and took us to inspiring speakers to calm our fears during hard times and helped to summarize the good times.

Patty Lopez who has been a walking advertisement for this work, brought many people to my classes and personally contributed to the creation of this book.

Lupe Diaz whose undying faith in my work compelled her to buy the first 125 copies of this book long before it was printed.

Manuel Camarena who has been an unfailing consultant and friend for many years.

Donald Peake who took it upon himself to bring this work to a higher level and filled many of my courses with his referrals.

Mike Packard who was always accessible as my genius volunteer consultant in every area from creating software and teaching me how to be friendly to my computer to supplying delicious teas and mugs.

Joel Roberts, the media coach and strategist who helped give me the language to present my work with succinct clarity.

To Samuel and Geraldine Sanzone whose love and guidance ring throughout this book.

I wish to make special mention of Carl and Roberta Deutsch whose touching and loving gestures toward me are equaled only by those I received from my father. Their thorough belief in me whose touching and loving gestures toward me are equaled only by those I received from my father. Their thorough belief in me and their sponsorship of several years allowed me to stay in this work when times were difficult and my faith weak. In fact, it was Roberta who gave me the computer with which much of this book was created and which I named "Robertita Deutsch."

I have been supported by many people who were not aware that they were assisting my writing, but their affection, encouragement and ideas were all my company in the solitary confinement of writing. Thank you all.

Dr. Edward W. Ablon, Nancy Ablon, Wendy J. Ablon, Stephen Adams, Denise Adams, Nelly Cañar Antich, Dr. Charles and Katherine Agnew, Olga Marina Aguilar, Carlos Aguilar Bolaños, Ann Ash, Cindy Aylward.

Monica Ballard, Masusa Barroso, Carmen Martinez de Beas, Bob and Stella Blomé, Gilda Bojorquez, Rebecca Brooks.

Dr. Dening Cai, Mimi Castillo, Giselle Chaghouri, Michel and Nahil Chaghouri, Cindy Chaouli, Lauren Chandler, Marianne Cheyne, Eliodoro Chavira Cevallos, Marina Ungo de Compte, Aviva Covitz.

Sherry Beall D'Ambrosio, Vito and Giovanni D'Ambrosio, Karina D'Arcy, Heather Daugherty, Daniel Deutsch, Ernesto Diaz, Pablo Diez, Magda Duran, Magda Pacheco de Duran, Patricia Dutriz.

Carol A. Eisenrauch, Gail Elen.

Lisa Fairchild-Jones, Jose Leon Flores, Gloria Rodriguez de Flores, Jessica Franzini, Daniel Fuentes, Roxana Fuentes.

Art and Nancy Galindo, Evelia Garcia, Charles Gohman, Keith Granate, John Gonsalves, Bobbie Grubber.

Julie Hamilton, Nikki Haught, Michele Hebert, Kathleen Helmer, Jim Helt, Myrtha Barberis Helt, Michael Henry, Christian and Colette Hope, Stephenie Hope, Paige Huff.

Gladys Duran de Iglesias, Faisal Ismael.

Jerry Jenkins, Al and Brighitta Jerumanis, Dr. Linda Johnston, Tom Justin.

Eric Kampmann, Kathryn Kern, Joe Kessler, Tere Macchia de Khoury, Jim Kozac, Steve Kroeter, Gail Kump.

Jorge Ruiz Bandini, Tere Ruiz de Ladron de Guevara, The Learning Annex, Sharon Leeds, Eileen Leizer, Lany Lippman, Karen Lentz, George and Vicki Lepisto, Susana A. Luna, Bettina Triulzi de Lopez, Frances Lopez.

Lic. Ana Maria Martinez Lavin, Nadine McGrath, Elena Mejia, Joan Miley, Graciela Minarrieta, Danielle Monahan, Ryan Monahan, Sean Monahan, Myreah Moore, Valborg Moore, Laura Morris, Steve Morris, Gloria Moss, Mariella Bustamante de Murillo, Carmen Elena Triulzi de Muyshondt.

Ammiel Najar, Moshe and Shannon Ninio.

Maggie O'Farrill, Marçeau and Yvette Olivier, Jim Oxford.

Feliciano Peña, Laura Peralta-Jones, Mayita de Perez Salazar, Phyllis Persechini, Sam and Gina Pilia, Nicole and John Pilia, Sor Maria de la Cruz Pinto, Andy Provenzano.

Michial Ratliff, Olga Reinoso, Alicia Duran de Restrepo, Diane Rivers, Stephanie Roderick, Nat Rubinfeld.

Col. Jose Luis Sanchez-Gomez, Alberto De La Sanchez, Corinne Sanchez, Rosita Castro de Santos, Frank and Sandra Sanzone, Kelley and Alexa Sanzone, Dr. Samuel Sanzone, Dr. Charles Schneider and Dori Schneider, Sandy Sessler, Graciela Speare, Ann Seymour, Gerardo Sol-Mixco, Rev. Tim Storey, Mimi Gramatky Stradling.

Alicia Tapia, Sheri Tarvin, Suzanne Taylor, Alberto Triulzi, Deborah Padget Triulzi.

Mariancita Urquilla, Martita Urquilla.

Sor Maria Elena Velasco, Gustavo Vicchi, Roger Vorst.

George Wade, Teresa Weaver.

Marta Monahan

To learn more about Marta Monahan and the
Marta Monahan Catalog of educational programs, books,
videos and merchandise, or to subscribe to the
Marta Monhan newsletter, please contact us today.

TEL: 310.235.1425
877.784.BOOK toll free from United States and Canada

FAX: 310.575.1868

EMAIL: info@vittoriomedia.com

WWW: www.vittoriomedia.com

Vittorio Media books may be purchased for educational,
business or sales promotional use.
For information please write: Special Markets Department,
Vittorio Media, Inc., 11601 Wilshire Boulevard, Fifth Floor,
Los Angeles, CA 90025